PRESENTING YOURSELF

A Personal Image Guide for WOMEN

PRESENTING YOURSELF

A Personal Image Guide for WOMEN

Mary Spillane

from the Color Me Beautiful Organisation

PIATKUS

*To the millions of women we have had the honour to help feel
more confident in making the most of themselves.*

© 1993 Mary Spillane
CMB is a registered trademark of
Color Me Beautiful Inc.

First published in 1993 by
Judy Piatkus (Publishers) Ltd
5 Windmill Street, London W1P 1HF

First paperback edition 1994

**The moral right of the author
has been asserted**

*A catalogue record for this book is
available from the British Library*

ISBN 0-7499-1308-8
ISBN 0-7499-1281-2 (Pbk)

Designed by Paul Saunders
Illustrations by David Downton
Photography by Iain Philpott
Photographs on pages 41, 43,
45, 47, 49 and 51 by John Steward
(See also Picture Credits on page 153)
Hair and make-up by Martin Fletcher

Typeset by Create Publishing Services, Bath
Printed and bound in Great Britain by
Bath Press Colourbooks, Blantyre, Scotland

Contents

Acknowledgements

I thank my entire London staff for their tremendous support given during the frantic months preparing this book, and in particular the incomparable Veronique Henderson for her organisational wizardry and having the nerve to argue with me enough so that the final result is CMB's best; Sue Abbott for her critical editing, and Trevor Castleton, my joint MD, for running things so smoothly in my absence.

Thanks also to our lovely models: Kate Cameron, Liz Baker, Pauline Brandt and Ruth Brooks who proved all the key points so professionally and with such style.

Diane Williams of Marks and Spencer; Mark Binnington of Next Directory; Pamela Lewis of Ken Lane, South Moulton Street; The World Gold Council; Fabrice Karel; Gary of Joel & Son; and Bally Shoes – all respected colleagues who supported this book with the loan of their beautiful clothes and accessories. Plus, I am indebted to Martin Fletcher whose artistic hair and make-up skills I employ on all major CMB projects.

Angie Michaels kept me alert on changes in US corporate image policies and practices and remains a dear friend as well as a most respected associate in image consulting.

Thanks also to Steve DiAntonio and the CMB/USA team for crediting their European counterparts with welcome innovations to colour and image advice now being used by Color Me Beautiful around the globe.

To Judy Piatkus, Gill Cormode and Philip Cotterell of Piatkus Books for seeing the on-going potential of CMB ideas, and to Heather Rocklin for getting them into shape for publication.

Finally, I must thank the entire team of CMB Image Consultants working in Europe, Africa, the Middle and Far East who continue to feed me with ideas for improving our services to meet the needs of today's women.

Introduction

This book is for and about **you** – and how you present yourself every day in your working life. How you look, how you behave and speak, comport yourself in meetings, give a presentation, is as important to your career advancement as your experience and capabilities. This book will help you find out if **your** image is working for or against you, and, in the latter instance, the many ways in which you can bring about improvements.

A poor image is self-defeating. It gets in the way of you projecting your true qualities and abilities. Many of us may *wish* this wasn't the case, that we should rather be assessed only on our achievements, not on additional, superficial factors such as appearance. But it is a fact of business life today, that **you** are an essential tool in communicating your ideas. How you 'package' or present yourself speaks volumes about how you value yourself and respect others, about your sense of quality, creativity and professionalism.

The advice I give is intended for women in large corporations as well as small enterprises, for women at the beginning of their careers, midway or returning after a break at home. It also attempts to cross national and cultural boundaries, and to be relevant for both profit-making and non-profit sectors.

YOUR PERSONAL IMAGE GUIDE

This book is for women and about the challenges we have in presenting ourselves in the workplace. I love speaking to mixed audiences on the subject of image, especially to air the concerns both sexes have about dealing with each other. But both men and women also want advice on more personal matters that they are less willing to discuss in mixed groups: body shapes, grooming and the like. So, in the following chapters, woman-to-woman, I can give it to you straight from the hip. The men have their own companion guide about presenting themselves more confidently.

This book explains why **you** are the message in business and public life, and how others read you. Whatever your image is today and no matter how well it may have worked for you thus far in your career, it might not be enough for you tomorrow, to project what's needed to help you succeed in new arenas.

You will learn how to develop an image that suits your present and possible future position, your lifestyle, and your own personality. Don't fear arbitrary prescriptions. There is no one winning formula: 'Buy this suit, wear this hairstyle, speak this way to be successful.' It is not that simple; nor is it difficult.

You will be actively involved in assessing your present image and how it measures up, whether you think yourself to be below, on a par with or even above your peers when it comes to projecting a confident, attractive image.

Learn what is special about you – and how to capitalise on your assets and play down any liabilities. Most women don't have perfect bodies, so we'll deal honestly with the challenges of needing to look your best, regardless of size. You will learn not only how to make the most of your present shape with clever camouflage tricks but also how to build healthy eating and exercise and, therefore, more energy into your busy life.

There are tips for handling yourself in meetings, and how to score points whether you are in the chair, a participant or presenting. Meetings are vital opportunities for you to show your capabilities, gain visibility and recognition.

If the very thought of standing on your feet to speak in public leaves you weak at the knees, read how you can impress your audience so much with your image, that what you say will be even more authoritative and persuasive. Learn whether your voice is enhancing your presence or sending out wrong signals – fear, underconfidence, or weakness. Once you've assessed any problems, read how to resolve them, following advice that has worked for thousands of talented women like yourself.

How appropriate is your image today for the industry you are in? Do you plan a career move soon that might require a different look? Read how you can and **must** fine tune your image throughout your career.

Perhaps you are one of the increasing number of women chosen to be their organisation's spokesperson. Or perhaps you harbour dreams of a public life. Tips for the high-visibility/high-flyers will help you get your image sorted out before that important TV interview or selection speech.

Writing from experience

How am I qualified to give such advice? I am an image consultant but also a business manager, strategic planner, speaker and trainer. This is career number three for me, the previous ones having been in government (US) and in management consulting. I have managed budgets of $50 million, directed staff numbering over 100 and am most proud of building from scratch a successful international organisation involving a consultant network of over 1,000. Like many readers, I am also a wife and mother, and in consequence have severe constraints on my personal time to get my own image together (despite it being my job to do so!).

I share my background to show that in addition to consulting many organisations, top multi-nationals and small companies, I have had personal experience of working in business and understand first-hand the challenges encountered as a woman in getting one's image right. When I began my professional career in the 1970s women, in particular, had little idea how to dress and groom themselves to be taken seriously. Nor were there any mentors advising us at our schools, universities, or in the personnel departments that hired us. We were the New Women, and we had a lot to learn.

I wince when I think of some of the outfits I put together when working as a lobbyist on Capitol Hill in Washington, and have no doubt that my appearance on many occasions prevented me from accomplishing what I intended. I looked very young for my age and was working in a predominantly male environment. But I was a serious professional and worked hard to prove it. I made no time for things as 'frivolous' as shopping for clothes or going to the hairdresser, let alone asked for advice on how I might develop a more effective image. Who could I have turned to for advice anyway? If I only knew then what I know now . . .

Image consulting

Coming to Europe in the early 1980s, I recognised the potential of a new service – image consulting – which had started in the US a few years previously. However, there was a problem: not only was 'image consulting' a new phenomenon but, while Americans might be mad keen on self-improvement, Europeans were loathe to admit underconfidence about anything. My battle was to be uphill all the way.

That was 10 years ago. Today, political parties as well as blue-chip companies seek our advice at Color Me Beautiful. Average men and women no longer consider a session with an image consultant is any stranger than going to a beautician for a facial or to a health farm for a welcome retreat.

The Color Me Beautiful network, of 1,000 specially-trained Image Consultants in 28 countries, is devoted to helping people feel more confident about themselves through the image they project. And it was their enthusiastic response that inspired my first book: *The Complete Style Guide*, written for women working in and outside the home, from teenagers to grandmothers.

My clients are also responsible for my taking time out to write a second book, this time about what it takes to look effective as well as attractive at work. After a seminar or personal consultation on how to develop an image, most of them take two or three key recommendations on board immediately. They might begin wearing better colours, try new eyeglasses or adopt a more flattering hairstyle. They win compliments from colleagues, and reinforcement from customers almost immediately, and this positive reaction spurs them on to learn even more about making the

Successful women learn the tricks to look their best

most of themselves. Their questions get deeper, more specific. They say they need a 'reference book on image', to which they can refer whenever a new situation arises or they are preparing for a career move. So, here it is.

Many clients return two or three times for a fine-tuning or a follow-up session to learn how to update their make-up or last year's wardrobe on a limited budget. Some ask for a personal shopping trip to see how to put CMB's advice into practice. There are few jobs which bring such satisfaction. We are in the business of self-esteem. We not only teach women how to dress, update their look, wear make-up more effectively, how to handle presentations and business/social occasions successfully; above all we give them the confidence to *be themselves*. For, as you will learn in this book, a successful image is not about people noticing your snappy suits or being dazzled by your accessories. It is about people noticing you first, almost unable to remember what you were wearing after you left but having the impression that you looked professional, attractive and successful.

Have I convinced you yet of the importance and value of a successful image? Read these testimonials from women who have been to CMB. They may have had doubts before their visit, but not any more:

'The fact that eight months after getting my "image overhaul" I've been promoted is no coincidence. My boss actually mentioned my new appearance (he actually said "Great style!" three times during my appraisal). Many thanks from a grateful CMB devotee.'

'For years I've focussed on the substance of my job, ignoring my style as irrelevant. How wrong I was. No wonder in the past when I looked a mess my presentations were a struggle. I'll follow your advice to the letter.'

'Your seminar knocked me for six. How was I so blind about the negative signals I was sending with my image? Your honesty was much appreciated. Within a week I've put all your key tips into play. Now I'm knocking them for six!'

Now it's your turn.

CHAPTER 1

You are the Message

Stop for a minute and ask yourself why you have bought this book? Perhaps a friend recommended it or maybe you were intrigued after flipping through. You may know someone who has been to Color Me Beautiful and has made changes that really worked for her.

Somewhere in you lurk questions about your personal image and the impact it is having on your career. How do you think you present yourself to the world? How do you think others judge you, particularly those who don't know you or who meet you for the first time? Have you ever stopped to think of what you want to project to others; which qualities you admire and would like others to immediately identify with you?

Imagine yourself having a coffee with a colleague at a café near the office. In comes the Managing Director of a competitive company for whom your colleague used to work. She joins you both for a few minutes. In that brief time, what impression do you think you made? If you wanted to look clever and creative how could you project that in a few minutes over coffee without being totally obnoxious and monopolising the conversation? How can others sense that you are reliable or efficient without a full report from your immediate boss? How can you look successful – and 'going places' – without bragging about your achievements?

The answer is via your image. Your dress, your grooming, your voice and your behaviour tell people a lot about you within minutes of meeting. We all size each other up and make judgments about each other's values, backgrounds and capabilities, using such indicators. If you dress very safely, without flair, will people think you are creative? If your voice is hesitant, your eye contact fleeting, will you be dismissed as under-confident rather than successful? If your nails are bitten, will you project being a disciplined professional? If you drink fizzy cola at 10 in the morning, will you look mature? How you look, how you speak, how you comport yourself sends out vital messages to say what you are about, how successful you already are and, to some extent, have the potential to be.

HOW OTHERS SEE – AND JUDGE – US

Don't think for a minute that I am suggesting that you can learn a few tricks and fool everyone that you are someone that you are not. Your image needs to reflect who you are, or who you know you are capable of being. What you project should be what you are about. If you can't fulfil expectations your image will collapse around you. But this does not mean that any shortcomings you may have can't be overcome. If you are terrified of speaking in front of people you can learn how to deal with the stress, how to prepare and how to deliver a good presentation. If your dress is indifferent you can learn how to dress better, to look smarter. If your parents didn't teach you the finer points of dining etiquette, you can learn how to navigate your way through a five course meal in a five star restaurant. A successful image is honest but also makes the most of who you are and gives you the confidence to be yourself in any situation.

Recent research in the UK by Robert Half Associates: Survey of UK Personnel and Financial Directors, 1992; in the USA by Herbert Knoll and Clint Tankersley, University of Syracuse, 1990, shows that image makes or breaks your chances of getting a job as well as getting ahead. Chief Executive Officers, Personnel and Managing Directors in America and Europe concur that even to hope for serious consideration for a job you had better look the part. In the UK, 93 per cent of top decision-makers, and in the US 96 per cent, agreed that personal presentation was the key factor in gaining employment. In today's highly competitive job market just being qualified, better still experienced, simply isn't enough to get the job you want. Employers are looking for more. The more senior the person, the more he or she said image was vital to job success and advancement.

A study based upon three years of research by the Center for Creative Leadership found that more attention to image was vital for women trying to break through the 'glass ceilings' that prevent them from reaching the top in their careers. Of the women 'derailed' from the fast track, 35 per cent were told that their poor image accounted for their problems.

When we asked Robert Half Associates to survey 300 top UK Personnel and Finance Directors, to probe further on the importance of image in a woman's career, 93 per cent said that a woman's personal image was very or extremely important to her career development and success. This is borne out by a recent update by the Center for Creative Leadership on *Breaking the Glass Ceiling*, which cites an impressive image as a factor for success in the careers of women who were able to advance in predominately male environments or in posts previously held by men. The overall image of top achieving women was 'stylish, sophisticated, businesslike and commanding'.

THE WAY WE SEE OURSELVES

Our image affects not only how others perceive us but, equally important, how we perceive ourselves. When you look good you feel more confident. A positive image affects your self-esteem, you value yourself more and enjoy reinforcement from others. On days you *don't* bother about your appearance, you are more likely to retreat from opportunities to stand out, to shine.

Your image affects your performance. If you look good – attractive, appropriate and fit – you get more recognition from others, not because of your clothes alone but because you look the part. Think about when you receive positive recognition at work: 'great presentation', 'you handled that situation well', 'you're looking fit', etc. Doesn't it make you feel great? If you feel that you performed well, have met expectations or surpassed them, don't you want to keep it up, do even better? This reinforcement process of a positive self-image is cyclical. A better image leads to improved self-esteem, which gives you more confidence, which encourages your performance, which earns you more recognition, which returns to bolster your self-esteem.

In our work as image consultants all too often we see the process working in reverse. Perfectly capable, talented and hard working women are stymied in their careers because their poor self-image and low self-esteem inhibit them from expressing themselves and getting the recognition they deserve. A negative image – dressing badly, poor grooming, being unfit, under-confident behaviour, lacking presence – can actually lead to a deterioration in performance and in some instances almost to paranoia.

This was illustrated in an experiment with two groups of female job applicants. Both groups of women were made up prior to the interviews but one group were told that an unattractive facial scar had been added when in fact they were made up without one, just like the other group. When they reported back from the interviews, those who thought they had a facial scar said that the interviewers were distant and put off by their scars. The interviews went badly with those who thought they had a scar appearing less confident and more anxious than those who knew they had none.

So, our appearance affects ourselves just as much as it affects others with whom we live, work and meet every day. What gets in the way of you feeling completely confident in yourself? What criticism have you taken from friends or colleagues about your dress, weight, skin, hair that has hurt you in the past? Have you tried to improve yourself, that is, your image, since starting your career? If not, can you afford to pull down the shutters and not deal with the barriers to your own success?

YOUR IMAGE AUDIT

This book presents an opportunity for you to take a long hard look at yourself and to be honest about what aspects of your image are letting you down in your career. In the following chapters we will focus on your appearance and how you might learn to make more of yourself, but first let's see which aspects of your image you are satisfied with and where you need help.

Tick how you rate yourself.

Image factor	A Liability	On a par with peers	Above average	First-rate
Quality of your voice	☐	☐	☐	☐
Communication skills (written & verbal)	☐	☐	☐	☐
Presentation skills	☐	☐	☐	☐
Social skills	☐	☐	☐	☐
Dining etiquette	☐	☐	☐	☐
Eye contact	☐	☐	☐	☐
Handshake	☐	☐	☐	☐

Image factor	A Liability	On a par with peers	Above average	First-rate
Posture	☐	☐	☐	☐
Fitness	☐	☐	☐	☐
Grooming (hair, skin, hands, etc.)	☐	☐	☐	☐
Dress/personal style	☐	☐	☐	☐
Manners	☐	☐	☐	☐

Give yourself **three** points for every category you have that is **first rate**, **two** points for every one you consider yourself to be **above average** and **one** point for every one where you are **on a par with your peers**. Obviously, you earn nothing for every liability.

◆ If you scored **less than 8** points, your image is killing you. How you have lasted in your job is a mystery.

◆ If you scored between **9 and 12** points, you are Ms. Average who offends few but scores little with people who count in your career – your current and future employers.

◆ If you gave yourself **13 to 24** points, you have tried in some respects to excel but present an inconsistent image – good in some aspects but weak in others.

◆ If you scored **25 to 36** points, you know that your image is important and have no doubt done many things to work on improving yourself. You may have had help from parents who instilled the importance of manners, dining etiquette or being well-dressed. But other aspects you had to learn either through special training, reading, or by being observant. Well done!

You deserve to have a first-rate image, one that earns you the respect and appreciation of others and, most importantly, gives you the confidence to be yourself. That is what this book is about – making the most of who you are and presenting yourself in the best possible light, at whatever point you may have reached in your professional life.

FINE-TUNING

You do need to be aware of how important it is to develop your image throughout your career. What works at one level, in one business, in one culture might not be appropriate or successful in another. The shrewd businesswoman assesses the intangible nature of new and different environments and makes the necessary adjustments not simply to fit in, but to succeed.

What follows are a few key events likely to occur in your career, any of which might be the major catalyst to do something positive to improve your image. All the necessary strategies for dealing with them are covered in greater detail in later chapters.

THE FIRST JOB INTERVIEW

What blood, sweat and tears go into that first CV. People pore over reference books, even take courses in presenting themselves on paper. But too few consider the importance of their personal image at a job interview.

I can hear all you students and young women sighing, 'But image costs money!' Indeed it does, initially. So, if you don't own an appropriate outfit, and can't borrow one from a friend, then a bank loan is in order. In a survey of top recruiters and personnel directors, the key factors that create a favourable impression at an interview proved to be:

1. **A smart suit**

2. **Looking fit and healthy**

3. **An attractive hairstyle**

4. **Being nicely made-up**

In later chapters, you will learn how to select clothes to suit both you and your budget and how to handle yourself in interviews. But the important thing here and now is to appreciate how vital your personal image is in the competitive job market, particularly when, without experience, you are selling only **yourself** and your potential.

YOUR FIRST SUPERVISORY JOB

This is your first opportunity to learn that the real challenges in business are sorting out the 'people problems' – from overseeing the processing pool to managing your former peers – now that you are higher up the corporate structure. Everyone knows it is your first chance at managing a team. Some will be nipping at your heels, attempting to undermine, but others will be genuinely rooting for you to succeed.

You are more likely to succeed if you are perceived to be working for the benefit of the team not just yourself. But you are not a team-player any more; you are the leader. And you need to convey your change in status subtly. This means looking more professional – no cardigans, only jackets; smart accessories colour co-ordinated to your outfit. Remember, too, that bare legs look unprofessional, and going without make-up looks unpolished. Set the standard for a smarter appearance for your entire team – be its members male, female or both.

Previously, you probably sat at the meeting table and waited for an opportunity to make your presence felt. Now you must set the pace, style and tone for your own meetings. Prepare, read, study everything you can in order to send the right messages to your team, as well as to those who had the confidence to promote you.

MANAGING A LARGER SCOPE

You've done so well that you are asked to take on broader and different responsibilities, but you still have lots to learn. Once the heady excitement of the appointment recedes, panic can set in if you aren't prepared.

Many at this stage foolishly try to bluff their way through; others determine to become the expert on everything, swotting up feverishly on every aspect of the new business. Neither route leads to success. Remember that people will need and want your leadership, so look in control while still welcoming help from your staff. Listen and learn. Without their co-operation you can't succeed.

Your communication and presentation skills are vital at this stage in your career. If you haven't learned how to relax and enjoy speaking to larger groups it is essential to do so now. Written communication is important but you'll have significantly more influence if you can speak to your staff, get their input, and debate ideas effectively. See Chapter 11.

Even under pressure don't let your personal image slide. It is essential that you look on top of things. Remember to eat sensibly and set aside time for some form of exercise in your weekly diary. Visit your hairdresser each month and don't forget your make-up. Most of us look colourless, badly groomed, and tired without any.

Get around and meet your new teams where they work. Visit the shops or factory floor. Impromptu visits are often the best opportunities to meet the real brains in an organisation, the people who can actually explain how things work, what really happens. Occasional meetings with the general staff are often better if in smaller groups and less formal than your management meetings. Encourage discussion by wearing more 'user-friendly' colours. See Chapter 4.

STARTING YOUR OWN ENTERPRISE

More women than men today opt to start their own enterprises. Often they have left a traditional organisation out of a need for greater flexibility in juggling the taxing roles of mother and partner, along with pursuing a career. In addition to the increased freedom, few professional opportunities are as challenging or potentially rewarding as building a business from nothing. Even so, initially it can be exhausting, and you will need to keep a very cool head.

You need to project an innate confidence to everyone on whom the new venture depends, including your financial backers/bankers, suppliers, potential customers, and your initial staff. All must believe that your idea has real potential. You believe it but they need to as well, if you are to survive.

As an entrepreneur, you can have more freedom in your mode of dress back at the shop or office. But when dealing with outsiders, revert to traditional business dress to inspire confidence. You may now manufacture leotards, but you are advised not to wear them when you meet with your backers.

Most start-up ventures are launched on tight financing. The first three years rarely pay dividends, often only a modest salary for the principal. This is when you can start to look dated and a bit worn, because every bit of spare cash gets earmarked for other necessities. But when you are launching a new service or product you have to look as fresh as your idea. That doesn't necessarily mean expensive clothes – just touches that show you are a woman of the moment, that you know what makes the market tick, have your finger on the pulse of your customers.

CHANGING JOBS

You change jobs when you get fed-up with the one you have or seek a greater challenge in your career. Whatever your motivation, these moves always contain an element of risk. You leave familiar territory where you know the business, where the staff and contacts know you, and know your worth which, for better or worse, makes life easier.

Changing jobs is one of life's most stressful experiences. You enter a new culture, need to learn your way. But most important, you need to sell yourself fast to make the transition as easy on yourself as possible.

You need to understand the culture and style of the organisation before you even go for an interview.

If possible, visit the lobby during a working day and see what people look like. Talk to anyone you know who has contacts within the new company, to try and get a feel for the environment. Find out not just what's in the annual report but what's in the press, who are their competitors and what are their present priorities.

To get the job, you need to look and behave as if you are already a part of that particular culture. All employers are looking for people to fit in, not to stick out.

Once there, you'll want to win as many supporters as possible while still projecting the authority of your position. Avoid being a clone of your predecessor; be your own person while taking care not to ruffle too many feathers. Set the tone early on, regarding how you like to deal with staff, peers and higher executives.

If your career is at the crossroads and you are considering a bold move, read this book carefully and you will learn everything you need, not only to win a terrific new position but to establish yourself quickly as a valued asset to the company.

RETURNING TO WORK

Having taken some time out from traditional work you no doubt harbour great anxieties about being accepted back into the 'real world'. Many women, who seek new challenges after raising a family, quickly find out how much things have changed in their absence.

The technological changes are mind-blowing enough, but you can deal with those by taking a refresher course offered through your local Adult Education programme. The real problem for woman-returners is that they can look 'out of date'. A personal image that was considered very acceptable even three years ago, can look very dated in today's offices. Observe working women on their way to work – notice how they are dressing today. What's changed? You will no doubt see that their hairstyles and accessories are different, along with the more significant changes in clothes.

Make your hair and make-up the first priorities for change, before you have that all-important interview. During spells at home, most women relax their grooming routines in lieu of more pressing matters, but the working world demands a certain polish. While investing in a new hairstyle, ask for instructions on how to take care of it yourself. And learn how to revise your make-up, using the most flattering colours and techniques to suit you.

Assume you will need one new 'high confidence' outfit for your interview. Chapters 4, 5 and 6 contain lots of ideas about selecting one that will not only make you look terrific but also be versatile in working with other items you already have or will purchase later.

Above all, keep things in perspective. You are a talented woman with plenty of managerial skills to apply once back in the traditional working world. You haven't been 'out of work' while at home, but simply working for different rewards. So get your image into shape by looking professional, and show them that you mean business.

REDUNDANCY

In recent years, few of us have escaped the impact of the economic recession that has plagued most developed countries. We've all known someone, perhaps in our immediate family circle, who has been devastated by being made redundant. We may also have been made redundant ourselves. Even though you can logically explain why you lost your job, such reasoning often does little to save your self-esteem.

Periods of being out of work can be liberating or they can be stressful. Much, of course, depends on your financial security. Also, the change of lifestyle often brings physical changes. Many redundant workers and their employers have sought help from CMB consultants to coach them in handling interviews. We notice that many gain or lose a lot of weight, so that their clothes no longer fit properly, but the last thing these people need to hear is that they must invest in a new suit, that fits.

If redundancy *has* hit you, try to keep your fitness up. Here's a great opportunity to improve your physical appearance as well as your spirits, so take up the gauntlet and get active. An active body keeps the mind active. You will enter those crucial job interviews looking less beleaguered, more energised. See Chapter 9 for more encouragement.

CHAPTER 2

The 'Right' Image

Today, we women are bombarded with advice about how we should look for work. Magazines, which purport to target us as readers, show attractive young model girls wearing trendy but devastatingly short or tight outfits that could be justifiably cited as sexual harassment by male colleagues if you wore them to the office. Real women in real organisations know that dressing in a way that is too provocative gets you nowhere but in trouble – and can make you look ridiculous. Why, then, do the magazines insist that this is how we should dress for work?

Last year, a leading British magazine for working women had a relaunch featuring a beautiful teenager with long blonde hair, and wearing a short, red, 'begging for a hug', knit dress. As striking as the image was, did they really think women who are managing men or have boardroom ambitions should dress like that? The magazine defended itself by saying that the image was one that many working women would *like* for the office.

Lots of women, if given the option, would *like* to wear tracksuits or jeans to the office but know they would not last a minute if they did. However, in America, a new craze for 'Casual Days' is taking hold in many companies. Once weekly or monthly, staff wear what they like. Many take great liberties and sport tracksuits, shorts and well-worn jeans. The jury is still out on the benefits of relaxing corporate dress-codes, but women who are keen on their career advancement are advised not to hurt their chances by taking too great liberties on company 'casual days'.

Few industries, even female-dominated ones, allow a woman to dress simply as she *likes*, although standards of work clothing for women only became a serious consideration about 20 years ago, post 'Liberation', and particularly in the 1980s, when more women than ever opted for careers outside the home or, indeed, were obliged by financial commitments to enter the workplace.

As increasing numbers of women now ascend to positions of power, we are told we can take a few more liberties. But look at any woman holding a boardroom post or a high political office and you will usually see the most conventional, classic business image. These women got to their present positions because they played safe, because they thought *professional* every time they bought clothing or accessories. Even so, there are variations to the classic suit that are not only acceptable but quite definitely preferable. While I could never recommend long flowing hair, mid-thigh hemlines and clinging knits for a successful business image, there are countless options in colour, style and accessories to make your working clothes more enjoyable and interesting than the array of uniforms that might be hanging in your wardrobe.

Before we get down to specific details, let's consider what is meant by a 'corporate image', how that relates to you in the workplace, and how you need to respond in order to climb the corporate ladder.

THE INDUSTRY, THE IMAGE

The business of image is integral to every organisation. Whether it is a multi-national conglomerate or a single-issue, non-profit group, a clear corporate image is essential for communication with customers, clients and the organisation's many constituencies. Without such a clearly defined image, a trader has difficulty projecting what the organisation is all about, what it offers and where it is going.

Consider some of the best-known, household names like Sony, Coca-Cola, Virgin, and MacDonald's. You can visualise their branding . . . MacDonald's golden arches; the red and white Coke cans. Customers can easily identify them on the high street, and in the supermarket. Other image statements are the company brochures, its advertising, the packaging of its products, its offices, factories and headquarters and, in some companies, the staff uniforms. All of these images add up to a composite picture of what the company is and where it is going.

YOUR CORPORATE IMAGE

Think of the buzz words used to describe *your* company or organisation. Maybe you have played a part in developing some of the corporate communication materials, the brochures or advertising. Or possibly you train new personnel in the corporate culture. What is your company trying to project to the outside world?

If your company says that its products are top *quality* but its service representatives dress in shabby, ill-fitting suits, will the claim be as believable as when those same reps are well-groomed and more presentable? If your services really are *professional* but the trainer you send to conduct a pilot course doesn't wear a suit, will you have the authority you hoped for with that client? If you say that your bank is really *friendly*, that people can come in and discuss their problems with your staff, yet most are dressed like police officers in navy suits and white shirts, do you think that invites people to share their problems and feel they are getting a friendly welcome? If you want to project that you are a *creative* and *forward-thinking* company, should your staff all look like clones of each other? Is your claim of *reliability* believable if your marketing managers look too trendy?

Many companies are increasingly aware of the importance of getting their image right, and have turned to CMB for advice on how their staff could make a better impression on clients and customers. Often there's a catalyst for change: a new management team comes in; a company wants to expand its export markets; or a department gets reorganised; companies and corporate cultures merge.

The following are a few examples of organisations going through a transition who considered the image of their staff needed some improvement.

Discussing how best to reflect the company's image can be a great team-building exercise

GROOMING WOMEN FOR THE TOP

Wanting to make more of the potential talents of their women, an international Bank designed a week-long course called Career Skills Development especially for female middle managers keen for a long-term career with the Bank. The week was (and still is five years later) a carefully designed potpourri of career planning workshops, role-plays to act out those difficult but typical situations with colleagues and supervisors, problem-solving with case studies, presentation skills, networking and negotiation skills, as well as image.

CMB were asked in because the Bank felt the women were damaging their chances for promotion and higher management jobs simply because of the way they dressed. We come in halfway through the course with the good news for these women, that they can 'fake it until they make it'. That's right: if their image is great, makes them look confident, capable, worth listening to, people will give them a hearing. That applies to you, too. The right look, coupled with a confident voice and matching behaviour or body language can win respect immediately.

Women love the advice, particularly when I tell them they should not look like clones of their male colleagues. Certainly, banking is serious business but women need to dress like women. Breakfast focus groups I've held with financial and personnel directors confirm that men feel uncomfortable with women who don't dress *differently* from men in business. They concur that women need to look smart, but urge them to still be women. Dressing like a woman in banking does not mean pink suits, voluminous hairstyles and heavy perfume. Be colourful, but keep your suits neutral, saving the colour for your blouses. Have an attractive hairstyle, but not one that is distracting. Smell fresh and clean but don't overpower any meeting with a scent so pervasive that it interferes with the work at hand.

FEMININE OR SEXY?

Too often women shoot themselves in the career foot by taking liberties with their image at work. Young, unattached women in their twenties, in particular, often confuse the workplace with the disco or wine bar and come to work dressed as if they are ready for a 'hot date'.

Public Relations is dominated by women professionals. It is a fast-paced business that requires lateral thinking and good communication skills – both of which many talented women possess. But several PR companies have despaired about their female staff looking unprofessional

left This look is too sexy for business. The more you show the less authority you have. That goes for not just the obvious things like your neckline, but also your arms and legs. Avoid dangling earrings, bangle bracelets, long-loose hair and stilettos if you want to be taken seriously

right The same simple shift dress can work for the office if selected in a longer length and always worn with a jacket

and sending all the wrong signals to both clients and the media.

One such company asked us to make over their entire staff – from the receptionists to the Managing Director. Without exception, all the staff looked attractive and trendy in the latest fashions. With an average age of 27, most were trim and wore short Lycra skirts; there were also plunging necklines, flowing hairstyles, dangling earrings, and knockout perfume. I told them that a lot of the effort they were putting into their accounts was being discounted and undervalued because they looked too sexy. If their clients were men, many would be wondering how high the skirt would rise by the end of the meeting, rather than concentrating on a business deal. If their clients were women, they would probably be resented. As for the company itself, busy professionals want people working for them to look as if their priorities are with the company, not with maintaining a fashionable, sexy image. There is a huge difference between looking professionally attractive – pleasant and respected by both sexes – and looking downright sexy and distracting.

The women were advised to concentrate on better fit and quality clothes. Fewer items in their wardrobe, of better quality and style, would be far more effective than a lot of trendy separates. All their skirts should have at least one inch 'give' so they didn't cling or rise so much when the women walked or were seated. Body suits should have necklines no lower than the top of the armpit, and always be covered with a jacket for client meetings. Light denier hosiery, previously abandoned by all in the summertime, was decreed a must. Finally, they were advised that high-heels, trendy platforms or Doc Martens should be replaced by stylish court-shoes or medium-heeled pumps.

When we had a review some months later, all reported how much easier it was to get down to business, negotiate fees and gain agreement on account plans now that they were so conspicuously 'professional'.

DIFFERENTIATING THE MANAGEMENT

In the hotel industry, many staff are uniformed. The job of selecting the best styles and colour combinations to suit the myriad of staff and the different positions is very challenging, so CMB are often asked to advise on colours that are flattering to most people, and project friendliness as opposed to projecting authority, as well as which styles are generally becoming.

One international hotel group prides itself on the wholesome values and strong ethical culture of its American founders. Despite being one of the world's largest hotel operators, the company's philosophy is based on quality, service and friendliness. 'The staff are there to take care of customers and to have fun doing it,' explained the Chairman. I was asked to deliver a seminar on personal image for the managers of the group's European, African and Middle East Hotels at a sales conference in Vienna.

After my presentation, it struck several of the managers that some of their key people didn't look as good as the front desk staff, who all wore smart uniforms. Some wore the same uniforms as junior staff and regularly ran into difficulty with business clients who insisted on seeing 'the top person' only to be told that they *were* already doing just that.

The London and Amsterdam hotels then booked seminars for their management teams, each presenting different challenges. In London, the managers looked too severe and boring. They had to be reminded that they were in the hospitality business and based in a large metropolis, entertaining business people from around the world. More colour was required from the women's suits and make-up, to the men's ties. The ever-so-comfy rubber-soled shoes needed to be replaced by smart court shoes to do the women's suits justice. And the penchant for dresses worn by most of the female managers required 'pulling together' with a classic jacket. The men needed to appreciate that a crumpled linen jacket was especially bad mid-winter.

In Amsterdam, the staff were all expensively dressed but too casual considering that their clients, again, were mainly businesspeople. They needed to look more professional – which you can only achieve with a suit. The women holding management positions were horrified by the suggestion that they polish-up their act. Few wore suits and most wore no make-up. They looked more as if they were having an afternoon off to go shopping rather than actually running the hotel. They received very similar advice to that given to their London-based colleagues.

What image works best?

The previous examples illustrate how companies and individuals have to rationalise what they feel is appropriate for best projecting the corporate identity through the personal image of their staff. I have talked about very different organisations with very different cultures. To understand better what some of these different images might be, here are some guidelines I use.

PLAY IT SMART

An organisation's size greatly influences the guidelines for personal image of the employees. Large companies, with more formal systems for communication and management hierarchy, lend themselves to the finest in traditional business dress, the formal business suit, good grooming and appropriate accessories.

There are, of course, exceptions – companies, for instance, whose organic growth came from a different business culture to begin with. Two notable examples familiar to many are the Body Shop and the Virgin Group (part of which Richard Branson eventually sold). The founders of both companies are iconoclastic, and despite being highly successful business people, they challenge many traditional business values and practices. Anita Roddick and Richard Branson are products of the 'swinging 1960s' generation and have ignored established business conventions. They don't have to play by the rules. They have made it in spite of them.

With their success and leadership they might even help to relax standards of business dress. But until their 'devil may care', anti-establishment images are accepted by more companies you are advised to follow the guidelines in this book, which are based on experience and research of what will help you to get ahead in your career.

So what should you wear if working for a small company, rather than a large one? Small companies form and prosper off the backs of a few dedicated people willing to wear many hats. Because everyone is expected to 'muck in' as needed, the image of employees needs to be easier, less

Only a minority of women and men make it to the top despite their image. Body Shop's founder, Anita Roddick, is a good example of one of the select few

severe than in larger organisations. If you are the Managing Director, you will get the extra effort from your staff if they recognise that you are 'one of them' in a sense, that you are approachable, as well as being 'in-charge'.

Women running their own companies need the authority of wearing a jacket every day but can team this with dresses or skirts and blouses. The matching jacket and skirt suit is 'heavy-duty' in small companies, and might better be reserved for meetings with your banker or the board – at which it becomes the essential wear.

TRADITIONAL OR PROGRESSIVE?

Rarely when I ask people to describe their corporate image do they include both of these attributes – either a company sees itself as traditional or as progressive. Generally, the traditional companies are well-established while the progressive ones are often new, and aiming to chip away at their more traditional competitors.

In business, it can be risky to be exclusively *traditional* or *progressive* in image. Those overly concerned with tradition might be perceived as being too stuck in their ways and not adapting to the changes in the marketplace or the developing needs of their customers. Certain professional firms fall into this trap; for example, it can apply to some solicitors, doctors, accountants. While they want to inspire confidence in having a wealth of experience, they also need to project that they are up-to-date with new innovations and services.

Traditionalists need to shake their foundations from time to time to be sure their image is current as well as professional. Women in these firms are almost invariably discouraged from wearing trousers. For variety, they might try instead knit ensembles in interesting colours, such as a smart but loosely-tailored, knitted jacket over a simple knit dress or a toning top and skirt.

Bear in mind, however, that firms that value being and looking *very* progressive can worry customers that what they are selling or preaching today might be redundant tomorrow. So projecting a balance is terribly important.

The younger the company, the more it needs to instill confidence in its staying power. It might offer the most up-to-date products or services, at the most aggressive prices, but it needs also to project reliability and resiliency. Hence, you are advised to be more sober and reassuring in your dress.

The more progressive the company, often, the younger the staff. If you are working in such a concern naturally you will enjoy the spirit of the venture but you should always play safe in your attire. All too many women in such situations take greater liberties, wearing shorter skirts, inappropriate (that is, too trendy) jewellery and shoes that are too dressy – even frivolous – rather than smart. The outfits may actually have cost quite a lot of money but they just look cheap in business and don't show the same professional 'commitment' as a good quality suit and a more 'classic' pair of earrings.

B USINESS TRAVEL ABROAD

If your business takes you abroad, be guided by the standards of the culture in which you are doing business, but that does not mean you have to dress like the natives. It *does* mean, in particular, observe any national or local rules on such issues as skirt and sleeve lengths.

Travelling abroad *is* more of a minefield for women. It is all too easy to look parochial: the short, tight skirts acceptable in France don't work in New York. The 'big hair-do' so necessary in Dallas would sabotage any deal in Tokyo. The clumpy boots so commonplace in Stockholm would look clumsy and unprofessional in Brussels.

If you have never visited the country before, and neither have any of your colleagues, play safe with a smart suit, not necessarily your most exciting, but rather one you would usually wear for a Board presentation. Wear real accessories if you own them; if not, try to borrow a good watch, pair of gold earrings and a good string of pearls. Wear your best shoes, current – not trendy – and in perfect condition.

GOING INTERNATIONAL

If you are part of an international company with staff from many different nationalities, your future advancement will depend greatly on your superiors' perception of how well you get along with others. Your own work group might all be nationals, but you are advised to spread your wings and become known throughout the organisation. Observe any characteristic differences in the dress of other nationalities. If they are ex-patriates do they look as though they are? Or have they adapted their image to look totally integrated into the company?

How well do you think your own image 'travels'? Ask yourself: if you were lined up on an identity parade, would people be able to tell that you are from London, New York, Frankfurt, Milan, Sydney or Tokyo? What are the signs that give your nationality away? Do those distinctions make you proud or uncomfortable when you travel or if you compare yourself to others in your international organisation?

My advice is to resist the temptations to wear things that give away your nationality. This is not to suggest that you shouldn't be proud of being British, German, Japanese, American or whatever but never appear so typically nationalistic that others will infer that you are parochial, and unable to adapt, or to understand and appreciate the richness of other countries, other cultures, other peoples.

Shop for your clothes at stores that stock international labels – not difficult to find these days. Experiment, within the bounds of advice, on making the most of yourself given in Chapters 4, 5, 6, 7 and 8. Pay special attention to those accessories valued by all nationalities – your watch, your attaché or brief-case, and your shoes.

Consult your international colleagues; encourage their views on your own image. Your goal is to dress and behave in ways that could travel anywhere and relate to anyone, in any country. Once you achieve this, you will be a prime candidate for advancement.

CHAPTER 3

Terrific Every Day

When I ask an audience of women what it takes to look terrific at work every day, I am greeted by responses that generally mean: you need lots of time and money.

I assume that you have limits on both – either because you're busy with your career, or working just as hard at home, or possibly doing *both* – that you probably don't have much time to read magazines, cruise the shops to see what's in fashion or search out pieces to co-ordinate with your wardrobe. No. You probably have only a couple of hours every month to plan and to shop for your wardrobe and only minutes every day to put it together. You may also have a tight budget, particularly if you're just returning to work after starting and caring for a family.

Think about the investment side of your image. You have lots of demands on your take-home salary – or you will have, once you get it – and your image can often fall way down the list of priorities. In fact, your image should be high on your list and be planned into your annual and monthly budgets. If you look as if you're ready to go places, the chances are that you will, and will be earning more money before too long. Think of the money you do spend from time to time, on replenishing your wardrobe – a pair of shoes here, a jacket there, some earrings and so on. If you kept tabs on how much you spent on this kind of 'drip-feed', unplanned and unbudgeted shopping, you might be shocked.

Your new goal will be to plan your wardrobe as you plan other investments, and to stop wasting money on ad hoc items that never work with what you already have. The starting point is to discover what suits you, then to assess your existing wardrobe to see if it measures up and finally, to develop a shopping priority list.

Let's begin by seeing how well your present image measures up.

DOES YOUR IMAGE MEASURE UP?

Y N

1. Do you spend less than 15 minutes getting ready for work in the morning (not including a shower)? ☐☐

2. Do you wear earrings every day? ☐☐

3. Do you go to the hairdresser at least every six to eight weeks? Ideally, every four weeks? ☐☐

4. Does your hair require more than 10 minutes each day to look terrific and appropriate? ☐☐

5. Do you wear coloured nail varnish which matches your outfits and/or lipsticks? ☐☐

6. Do you manicure your nails weekly? ☐☐

7. Do you wear make-up every day to work or only when you go for an interview? ☐☐

8. When you sit down, does your skirt ride up several inches? ☐☐

9. Do you touch-up your make-up at all during the day? ☐☐

10. Do you know the difference between 5 and 20 denier? ☐☐

11. Is your wardrobe mainly comprised of navy, grey and other neutral colours? ☐☐

12. Do you wear a belt with your skirts (even if they don't have belt loops)? ☐☐

13. Do you know your most flattering skirt lengths for business? ☐☐

14. Do you know which styles make you look most trim? ☐☐

15. In the summertime, do you wear sleeveless dresses and blouses to keep cool? ☐☐

16. If you are petite, do you wear high heels to look taller? ☐☐

17. Are all your work shoes stored away in the wardrobe on shoe trees? ☐☐

Y N

18. On a day when you have an important meeting, do you dress differently?

19. Do you have a suit/dress and accessories – a special look – ready in the wardrobe for business dinners?

20. Are your shoes, handbags/attaché or brief-case and watch of good quality that projects your position and your success?

ANSWERS

Give yourself a point for every correct answer.

1. No.
Wash 'N' Go is a clever name for a shampoo but disastrous if it describes the amount of effort you put into your image each day. Your make-up and hair needs 15–20 minutes, with dressing and accessorising taking another 10. So a half-hour is the minimum goal. See also Chapter 8.

2. Yes.
Earrings are equivalent in importance for a woman to a tie for a man. See also Chapter 8.

3. Yes.
Your hair grows at its own rate but letting it go any longer than eight weeks without attention is letting your grooming down. See also Chapter 8.

4. No.
Hairstyles needing more than 10 minutes' care each day are only an option for single women who are early risers. Make life easier for yourself by investing in a cut and treatment that makes you look your best with minimal effort. See also Chapter 8.

5. No.
Coloured nail varnish is for women working in fashion or beauty. Otherwise it's a distraction and does nothing to project a woman who means business. Stick to buffed nails, or clear or light neutral varnishes. See also Chapter 8.

6. Yes.
The hands and nails are integral to your daily communication. Attend to them weekly at a minimum. See also Chapter 8.

7. Yes.
Women who wear make-up earn more and get promoted faster. Learn

how to wear colours that look natural and understated at work. See also Chapter 8.

8. No.

If your skirt sneaks up your thighs when you sit down, it is too short or too tight. Aim for an elegantly looser fit in skirts and trousers that stay where you want them to and are flattering not figure-hugging. See also Chapter 7.

9. Yes.

If you apply your make-up well in the morning (using CMB's 10-minute foolproof routine) then all you need to do is refresh your face with a little powder at lunchtime and touch-up your lipstick two or three times, depending upon how much you are on show that day. See also Chapter 8.

10. Yes.

If you don't know the difference between sheer denier hosiery and varying degrees of opaqueness you are probably diminishing the overall impact of your outfits. Get the thickness, density and texture appropriate for your wintertime and summertime wardrobes. See also Chapter 8.

11. No.

Neutrals are the mainstay of every working wardrobe but be sure you aren't playing so safe that your image screams 'BORING'. See also Chapter 4.

12. Yes.

A belt finishes off your skirts and trousers. A good quality one in a neutral tone that co-ordinates with most of your shoes can work with most outfits. See also Chapter 8.

13. Yes.

Forget what the catwalks are showing; find out the range of options available to make you look your best. If you don't know what lengths are best, some of your skirts are probably making you look dumpy while others are downright unattractive. See also Chapter 5.

14. Yes.

For jackets, dresses, skirts, trousers – consider cut, fabric, texture and patterns. Consider the mistakes in your wardrobe. Some of these clothes make you look heavier than you really are. Why? If you don't know, time to find out. See also Chapter 5.

15. No.

Sleeveless dresses inspire little confidence in your authority. Always keep your arms covered, at least to just below the elbow, and wear a jacket to any important meeting whatever the temperature. See also Chapters 6 and 7.

16. No.
High heels make most women, short or tall, walk awkwardly. It is true that, if petite, flats don't enhance your stature but a medium heel, say $1\frac{1}{2}$ inch, makes you look lovely and allows you to walk comfortably and elegantly. See also Chapter 8.

17. Yes.
If your shoes are in a jumble under the bed, or strewn throughout the house, you aren't getting the best return on your investment. Shoe trees can extend the life of decent shoes for YEARS. Also, in the cupboard, shoes do not collect dust and discolour as they can if left in daylight. See also Chapter 8.

18.
The answer should be **yes** or **no**. You want to fine-tune your look for effect for special meetings but should be consistently well-dressed so that you could handle any impromptu meeting with someone important. See also Chapter 10 and 11.

19. Yes.
Many working women under-estimate the importance of business/social events such as the drink or dinner after work. Plan for a look that can take the day into the evening elegantly. Freshen up your make-up and add a nice scent to enhance your image. See also Chapter 8.

20. Yes.
Why spend good money on your suits but practise false economy on your shoes? Make sure you 'finish off' your image with the best quality accessories you can afford. You deserve nothing less. See also Chapter 8.

◆ If you scored **15** to **20** points, your image is quite together. You know that you need to bother every day to make a good impression and are putting in the necessary effort. This book will help you fine-tune your image and let you explore new possibilities for looking even more successful.

◆ If you scored **10** to **15** points, your image is probably tired. You are not projecting as well as you need to do in order to get as far as you are capable. Time to rethink your business image and bring yourself up-to-date. This book will guide you on all aspects; study the details on grooming and accessories, which may be your weak points.

◆ If you scored under **10** points, your image is hurting your career prospects. Unwittingly, you are being inconsistent and sending the wrong signals to people who matter. You need to start from scratch. Follow the tips in this book, and you will find that a Successful Image is both easy to achieve and affordable.

WHAT IT TAKES

Now that we've examined the sort of situations in which you might wish to change or fine-tune your image, and the business considerations you need to keep in mind, it's time to concentrate on how to make those changes. The guideline we at CMB use to help women understand what it takes for any individual to project SUCCESS, is that you must first define what is unique about yourself in terms of colouring, build, personality and lifestyle. Then you must adapt your individuality to conform to your position, organisation/sector and culture. This formula produces a unique look for every woman, since no two individuals are exactly alike on all counts.

In the following chapters we will deal with your physical characteristics – your colouring and your build – and discuss how you can develop an image that is appropriate as well as attractive, but most of all: *yours*.

CHAPTER 4

Start with Colour

Colour is where we, as Image Consultants, begin when advising women on how to make the most of themselves. Colour not only affects how healthy and attractive you look, but also affects how you feel.

You probably have at least one or two colours in your wardrobe that make you look and feel like death warmed-over. Every time you put on a particular jacket or dress, you sigh and reach for your blusher and lipstick. The colour seems to drain you. It simply *wears* you.

Also, when you open your wardrobe, can you see any relationship between the colours? Just look at the colour families you have assembled there. Do you play it safe with lots of the same shades? Or is your wardrobe a veritable riot of colour, with lots of items seeming to scream for attention, not wanting or able to work with anything else?

Face up to it: as a busy working woman you can't afford to look miserable, overwhelmed or insignificant in the wrong colours. Nor do you need the hassle of trying to mix and match things that you bought separately, just hoping they'd go with *something* you already had – only to be bitterly disappointed. What you need is a system to make you look wonderful, to unclutter your wardrobe and to make shopping a snap.

COLOUR ANALYSIS

Millions of women (and men) have turned to Color Me Beautiful for advice on finding their best colours. We analyse what is special about your colouring – your natural skin tone, eye and hair colour – and advise you on which one of 12 colour palettes will make you look your best. We use the seasons of the year to describe people, and in my recent book,

The Complete Style Guide from the Color Me Beautiful Organisation, the twelve seasonal types (there are three types within each of the four seasons) are presented in detail.

Here I'll simply give you a basic understanding of how to develop a working wardrobe, using a personal colour theme.

DEFINE YOUR OWN COLOURING

Take a look at yourself in the mirror without any make-up, and with a bare neck and chest. How would you describe your colouring? Forget what you looked like when you were younger, and concentrate on your present colouring – unless you colour your hair, in which case consider the colour it is naturally.

Would you say your colouring is **strong and deep?** Women with dark hair and eyes fit into this category, and look wonderful in black and bold colours, such as red, purple, emerald green and royal blue. Or are you, by contrast **light and delicate**, almost translucent, in colouring. Blue-eyed blondes, and some women with very light grey hair are most suited to lighter colours. Then there are the women who project a real **warm and golden** glow. The redheads, women who freckle easily look wonderful in warm shades. So do the women with mid-brown hair that often has reddish highlights. Their opposites are the **rosy and cool** types, who have pink undertones to the skin, and no real warmth in the hair, which can be a beautiful grey to mid- or mouse-brown. Other women are best described as **bright and clear**; what you notice is the contrast between their usually dark hair, bright eyes and clear skintone. And finally, there are women who usually say they are 'mousey.' They know a lot of bright colours are unkind to them. Their colouring is **soft and muted** and so too should be the colours they wear.

On the following pages are examples of the different wardrobe options and make-up colours based on these six dominant types of colouring. Please note that I have not recommended specific colours for your foundation liquid/creme, as this is too individual; some colours are worn by many seasons. It seemed best therefore to limit advice to colour cosmetics such as lipsticks and eye-shadows. See which description of a type fits you best. Don't be swayed by the wardrobe that most nearly resembles your present one, as you may be dressing in colours that really aren't making the most of your natural colouring. For more details on finding out which of the 12 seasonal types you are, refer to *The Complete Style Guide*.

THE DEEP WOMAN'S WARDROBE

Overall Look:
Projects strength
Hair:
Black, brunette, dark auburn, salt 'n' pepper
Eyes:
Brown or hazel
Skintone:
Ivory, rich beige, dark olive, bronze black
Famous examples of Deep Women:
Whitney Houston, Joan Collins, Isabella Rossalini (left), Ruby Wax, Whoopi Goldberg (far left), Tracey Ullman, Caryn Franklin
Color Me Beautiful seasons:
Deep Autumn or Deep Winter

GENERAL WARDROBE GUIDELINES

Build your wardrobe on strong neutrals such as black, charcoal or navy. But always offset them with vivid colours: royal blue, red, bright yellow, turquoise to name a few. You are all about contrast, so wear light with dark as opposed to blended monochromatic tones.

Pastels are sickly on you. If you want to wear lighter colours, think *white* with just a hint of colour. We call them icy shades – the lightest pinks, blues and lemons. But these light colours are best reserved for blouses or sportswear, not for the office as a major item like a dress.

Your colours are rich, say mahogany, purple, olive and pine green, as well as primary and clear. To make the most of your natural colouring, be bold.

COMPLEMENTARY MAKE-UP

Rich lipstick colours, such as true red, when you wear your red. But for everyday lipstick and blusher try a translucent burgundy or cinnamon (choose the former if you know cooler/blue-based colours are your best, or the latter if warm tones flatter you). Don't neglect to complement the rich colouring of your eyes. Enhance them by framing them with a strong eyeliner – charcoal, plum, sage or brown (black is too severe) and by using soft neutral eye-shadows, such as pink and grey (if you are cool-toned) or peach and sage (if warm-toned).

THE LIGHT WOMAN'S WARDROBE:

Overall Look:
Delicate and translucent
Hair:
Blonde or light grey
Eyes:
Blue, blue-grey, aqua, light green
Skintone:
Fair – ivory or porcelain, peachy
Famous examples of Light Women:
The Princess of Wales (right), Selina Scott, Patricia Hodge, Linda McCartney, Melanie Griffiths, Tina Brown
Color Me Beautiful seasons:
Light Spring or Light Summer

GENERAL WARDROBE GUIDELINES

Your investment neutrals range from camel, stone and taupe to soft blue-grey and light-navy. Avoid dark, draining colours such as black or charcoal, which only make you look pale and insipid. Your white is ivory but better to opt for soft pastels such as apricot, buff, lemon, rose pink or sky blue when you need to offset your strongest colours like navy.

Have fun with bright colours, but be sure not to go too *electric*. Rather than a strong, royal blue try a clear, medium blue. A rich purple might overwhelm but if you mix with blue to make periwinkle you are on to a winner. Blue-greens are particularly nice on light women, and are very user-friendly colours.

Your red is best if clear, not too blue or deep. Mango or salmon pinks are fun alternatives when you want a new jacket to brighten up your basic skirts and trousers.

COMPLEMENTARY MAKE-UP

For everyday lipstick and blusher try a salmon or warm pink (if you know these warm tones look the most natural on you), or a plum rose (if you know the bluer-tones are your best). Avoid wearing frosted or pearlised lipsticks, which are too light and sporty for business; matt, medium shades are best for business. Define your eyes but not too strongly. Try a teal, grey or navy liner. For shadows: apricot or champagne with cocoa or soft grey will work with your whole wardrobe.

THE WARM WOMAN'S WARDROBE

Overall Look:
Golden
Hair:
Strawberry blonde, red or auburn
Eyes:
Topaz, hazel, warm green, teal blue
Skintone:
Ivory with freckles, golden brown,
peachy porcelain, yellow beige
Famous examples of Warm Women:
Duchess of York, Emma Thompson
(right), Shirley McLaine, Jennifer
Saunders, Rula Lenska, Angela
Lansbury
Color Me Beautiful seasons:
Warm Spring or Warm Autumn

GENERAL WARDROBE GUIDELINES

Some traditional 'business' colours, such as some greys and navies, are difficult for you. They don't make the most of your natural colouring. Instead, invest in golden browns, olives, camels and rusts, which are eminently professional and much more effective with your colouring.

Look for yellow, red or green undertones to your colours. Avoid white; instead, wear cream or buff. Choose a brick red rather than burgundy. Your blues are best if 'warmed up' with green – teal blue, for example.

You will look your most exciting if you think of an autumn landscape and put together blended golden tones like moss greens, mustards, terracotta and warm browns.

Black is not recommended unless it is kept clear of your face, that is, in your skirts or trousers. But it won't work with all the other wonderful golden tones in your wardrobe. So why buy it?

COMPLEMENTARY MAKE-UP

Terracotta or cinnamon lipsticks and blusher will work with your whole wardrobe. When wearing red, match yours with a rich brick red, always avoiding blue-toned reds like the plague. Your eyes will look best if framed with a coffee or moss green pencil or teal blue if you have blue eyes. When applying eye-shadow, dust your eye-lids with apricot or light gold, and strengthen with a bronze, copper or brown shadow.

THE COOL WOMAN'S WARDROBE

Overall Look:
Rosy – not light or dark
Hair:
Ash brown or blonde, or grey
Eyes:
Blue or brown (whose previous dark hair is now grey)
Skintone:
Pinky, rose-brown, beige, medium olive
Famous examples of Cool Women:
Barbara Bush, Germaine Greer, Anne Diamond, Joan Baez (right), Joan Plowright
Color Me Beautiful seasons:
Cool Summer or Cool Winter

GENERAL WARDROBE GUIDELINES

Steer clear of most browns, beiges, khaki and cream tones. Your cool colouring looks freshest in blue- or pink-based colours. Great neutral foundations are navy and charcoal but soften their usually severe impact when they are worn with white and team them instead with mauve, pastel blue, rose pink or soft fuchsia.

Pastels are wonderful for your blouses, dresses or jackets. However pastels in a complete outfit aren't strong enough for work, so they are not good choices for a suit. Over an aqua shift dress try a navy swing or 'cardigan' jacket.

Your red has a blue cast to it. The burgundies will work but test options out to ensure they aren't too ageing.

Very sharp or bright colours can overpower you. Aim rather for richness and subtlety.

COMPLEMENTARY MAKE-UP

Light lipsticks will make you look older, so yours should match the intensity of your eyes. Brown-eyed Cool women can go for rich blue reds and plums for lipsticks and blushers, while blue-eyed women of this type are better in softer, rose pinks.

Dust your eye-lids with soft pinks and define with grey, navy or plum shadows. The same colours for eye-liners will frame your eyes best.

THE CLEAR WOMAN'S WARDROBE

Overall Look:
Bright and contrasting
Hair:
Black, brown or rich grey
Eyes:
Steel blue, green, clear hazel or rich brown
Skin Tone:
Porcelain, ivory, dark ash brown, clear yellow beige
Famous examples of Clear Women:
Princess Caroline (far left), Elle McPherson, Pauline Collins, Oprah Winfrey (left)
Color Me Beautiful seasons:
Clear Spring or Clear Winter

GENERAL WARDROBE GUIDELINES

Use light and dark colours mixed together, or one bold colour on its own. Black, charcoal, royal blue and red will be basics you can mix with many other shades to look your best. Soft monochromatic blends, so elegant on others, will be boring on you regardless of the price or designer label.

Your striking colouring can overwhelm other people particularly if you limit your colours to strong neutrals such as black and navy. Lighten your impact by using more colour near your face. A bright yellow scarf or jacket will take the 'hard' edge off a black dress. Hot pink makes navy more feminine but still business-like.

Taupe and pewter can lighten up your summertime wardrobe but never team with light colours; look to your primaries instead.

COMPLEMENTARY MAKE-UP

Your colouring is bold; so, too, must your make-up be. True red, strawberry or hot pink will complement most of your wardrobe. Test plum (cool-toned) versus salmon (warm-toned) blushers to see which is most natural on you. Your eyes should be the centre of attention so always define them. Match your shadows and eye-liner with the intensity of the colour of your eyes: softer shades if you are blue-eyed (for example, an opal pink with charcoal or navy) and stronger shades if you have hazel or brown-eyes (try, for example, apricot with plum or spruce).

THE SOFT WOMAN'S WARDROBE

Overall Look:
Blended and muted
Hair:
Medium grey, mid or 'mousey' brown,
ash blonde
Eyes:
Blue green, brown, grey blue
Skintone:
Ivory, rose or yellow beige, light olive
Famous examples of Soft Women:
Hillary Clinton, Joanna Lumley, Amanda
DeCadenet, Jerry Hall, The Princess
Royal, Cindy Crawford (right)
Color Me Beautiful seasons:
Soft Summer or Soft Autumn

GENERAL WARDROBE GUIDELINES

These women aren't obviously dark or light but somewhere in between. Bright colours are harsh on them but that doesn't mean they are limited in looking wonderful.

If you fit this description, your colours need to be rich and blended. Monochromatic dressing when you use the same hue, but in lighter and darker values, is your most wonderful look. For example, you could try ivory, taupe, pewter and bronze mixed together. Something as stark as black and white would overwhelm your soft, subtle colouring.

Your pinks can either be the rose or raspberry tones, if your skin is cool (that is, pinky) or muted salmons if your skin is better complemented by warm colours (that is, more golden or creamy).

COMPLEMENTARY MAKE-UP

You need make-up to look alive but often despair at looking 'too made-up' when you experiment with strong colours. Your make-up must be soft and blended. Nothing too dark or too light for your lipsticks or eye-shadows. For every day, terracottas (if warm-toned skin) or plum rose (if cool-toned skin) will be your most attractive in lipsticks and blushers.

Reject colourful eyeshadows in favour of neutrals, to make the natural colours in your eyes 'come forward'. Try soft cocoa, grey or slate blue with a soft non-coloured highlighter, such as a pale melon.

USING COLOUR FOR EFFECT

Once you know which colours make you look best, naturally you'll want to learn how to use your palette strategically; different shades on different days to create different effects. What's needed for a tough presentation to the board will be wrong for a staff meeting at which you might want to find out what's troubling your people. So here's some advice on using colour to your best advantage.

PROJECTING AUTHORITY

Would you have much confidence in a judge who wore orange robes or a policewoman who wore a pink uniform?

No, we've been conditioned to accept that certain colours and images project authority whilst others can achieve the exact opposite. When in doubt, think 'sober and classic' when it comes to colour to project authority, particularly in male-dominated industries such as finance and law. Every woman's palette has neutrals such as navy, olive, grey and pewter. Offset a neutral suit with a colourful blouse. Your white will project the most authority but can look too boring when teamed with safe neutrals. You might opt instead for one of your pastels or primaries making sure its effect is elegant, not insipid or too electric.

In situations when you particularly need to project power try a solid jacket or suit in rich red, deep blue or royal purple. These three colours have been used so extensively by women in recent years that they are almost categorised as new neutrals and convey confidence in who you are. Other colours like pinks, yellows, greens, browns, oranges, no matter how flattering they may be on you, won't project the image you want, when you need to say: 'I'm in charge, just in case any of you are in doubt!'

COLOUR CUES

Colour response research shows that mid-tone colours, particularly warmed greys and browns such as stone, pewter and camel are the most user-friendly colours. That is, they are perceived as the least threatening and are therefore the most effective in getting people to open up and speak their minds.

So for that meeting when you want people to share ideas or problems, don't wear your brightest colours or very bold contrast. Your choice that day should be an insignificant colour that, if asked, people might not even remember that you wore. Pewter, medium grey, bronze, camel, stone and taupe are good colours in which you can look approachable, not threatening.

Wrong: Traditional business colours like navy and white can make you look pale, tired and overwhelmed if they don't suit your colouring

Wrong: No matter how pretty or flattering a colour might be, it must also look professional. Pastel suits and floral patterns rarely look right in business and lack authority

Right: To look authoritative, select a deep colour from your personal palette (see pages 40–51) and offset it with ivory, white or a complementary pastel

Every woman should know her best collegial colours to wear on days when she needs to win friends and influence people

FEMININE YET PROFESSIONAL

Businesswomen – like businessmen – come in many shapes, sizes and personalities. Some women are more 'feminine', more romantic by nature and are depressed if restricted to wearing very masculine, neutral colours, even though these are bearable to many other working women.

However, some very 'feminine' women jeopardise their career prospects because they take their natural preferences too far and wear colours and styles that are simply inappropriate in a business setting. Different industries and different countries all set limits as to what is acceptable for women to wear. In professions and industries still predominately run and staffed by men, women are cautioned not to give free reign to their feminine urges and buy suits or dresses in colours that stand out too much, that is, that are too light or too insipid – some pastels, for instance. Summertime is when many women fall victim to the tempting array of fashion suits in luscious pastel 'sorbet' shades. Resist them and choose instead medium-toned colours in lightweight fabrics, to look both elegant and appropriate.

If in doubt about a colour's appropriateness, ask yourself what the likelihood would be of one of your male colleagues being accepted in something very out of the ordinary, such as a light-coloured suit when the rest of his colleagues are more soberly attired. Certainly, men have more limitations on colour when considering what is acceptable and professional. But if you are seriously ambitious you cannot afford to disregard those limitations yourself.

If you need consolation, remind yourself that pale or bright-coloured suits would make your dry-cleaning bills soar, and such treatments would soon cause the fabric to deteriorate. And because such a suit is more distinctive, people are more likely to notice if you wear it regularly, whereas a more neutral one can be accessorised in many different ways. It really is a question of moderation paying greater dividends on every score.

CHAPTER 5

Working with your body

Consider your current wardrobe. Which clothes do you enjoy wearing most often? If you are like most women, with a mixture of successes and disasters in your wardrobe, you wear 20 per cent of your wardrobe 80 per cent of the time. Wouldn't you love to be able to get up in the morning and grab anything, knowing it is going to fit, feel comfortable all day and look terrific? Well, it isn't an impossible dream, but you will have to work at it – and in addition to wearing colours that complement your colouring, you will also need to learn which styles complement your body.

RECOGNISING YOUR BODY SHAPE

An exercise I set during many of my seminars is to ask women to draw an outline of their bodies. Heaving a heavy sigh, with markers poised over a blank piece of paper, they set to work. Within minutes the giggles start, particularly when they start peeking at their neighbours' images. I do an outline of myself. This is what it looks like:

I have been told by reliable, unbiased sources that I don't actually have a head like a brick bunker nor legs like a duck. But that's how I see myself, when I look in a full-length mirror, unclad.

All women can give you an immediate listing of their physical inadequacies: 'To begin with, I am overweight. My thighs are enormous, my neck too short and my arms better left covered at all times.' And so on . . .

Few women have perfect bodies and most are sensitive about their shortcomings, real or imagined. No doubt you feel that you have a few, too – but they should not be allowed to overwhelm you so that you can't get on with your life and your career. Simply face up to your body basics and then learn which styles are most flattering and what are the best options for you to consider for work.

In my previous book, *The Complete Style Guide*, I devoted 25 pages to a discussion of the Seven Basic Body Shapes we at CMB use to help women understand *their* basic shape. When women think about their shape they often think only of the lumps and bumps, or where they are widest; understandable, but demoralising and not appropriate. Instead, you should start by determining which of the following shapes is nearest to your own:

◆ An angular shape – like a rectangle with no waist and fairly flat hips and bottom.

◆ A curved shape, with a defined waist, and rounded hips and bottom.

◆ A combination of angles and curves: straight shoulders, definite waist and curvy bottom.

◆ A full-figured round body, often combined with a short waist and long legs.

Remember, when trying to assess your body shape, do so from the front as well as the side. You might look quite full or round from the side but have quite a flat or straight silhouette from the front. If your bust and hip measurements are ample it does not necessarily mean that you are Curvy. Your bottom may be flat and although your hips are wide, they will look better in neat, undarted styles. What you should check is the extent to which there is definition between the zones, how defined your waist is, how indented the small of your back is, if your hips and bottom are flat (be they 36 inch or 56 inch) or if they are rounder, more curvy.

Once you have determined your basic shape, just check out your options, accordingly, in the following sections.

THE ANGULAR WOMAN'S CLOTHES OPTIONS

Now let's consider a woman who has a straight, angular body. She wants to change her look, and goes shopping for a dress to go under some of her jackets. After some deliberation, she buys a silk one with a gathered waist. Now, no matter how much she has spent on the dress, it will look

Angular figure

inexpensive and unsuccessful on her because such a soft fabric does not compliment her straight body. She would look much more interesting in a tightly woven material, such as a silk-linen blend or fine wool crêpe. Also, identifying a waistline which, in essence, she doesn't have doesn't do her figure justice. A better choice would be a chemise style or a coat-dress, with no waist emphasis.

If you have decided that your body shape is essentially Angular, then here are some tips on selecting styles that make the most of your features.

Silhouettes

• Simple and unconstructed • Straight lines • Square shoulders (regardless of padding) • Waist-definition (only if you have one) • Tailored and tapered designs

Fabrics

• Crisp cottons and linens • Wool that retains its shape, e.g. gaberdine, twill, tweed • Tightly woven knits and jerseys • Silk that's stiff (e.g. raw silk), blended with linen • Blends of natural and man-made fibres with body, i.e. which don't drape excessively

Details

• Sharp lapels, e.g. peaked or notched; asymmetrical • Edge to edge closings • Lapel-less jackets • Minimal darts or tucks at the waist (unless yours is defined) • Stiff or pressed-down pleats • Straight, cross-over, wrap-around, slit, knife-pleat skirts

Patterns

• Stripes of all widths • Fine to moderate polka dots • Plaids or geometric weaves • Modest paisleys • Abstracts that are more geometric in shape

THE CURVY WOMAN'S CLOTHES OPTIONS

If you select styles that are complimentary to your build, you will look your best, feel comfortable and even look slimmer. Consider the woman with a very feminine, curvy body: a full bust line, nice waist and full hips. In shopping for a business suit she buys a very smart Chanel-style with a short body jacket in a crisp wool gaberdine. The suit is the right size, and she has chosen a great colour for her. But she doesn't look good in it, because both the style and the fabric are wrong for her body type. Stiff fabrics, straight lines in jackets and skirts, and boxy cuts, make a woman

Curvy figure

57

with a soft, curvy shape look chunky and shapeless. Her lovely bust line, trim waist and feminine hips are all lost in a style like this.

Women with curvy shapes, and wanting to make the most of themselves, should select from the following:

Silhouettes

• Defined at the waist   • Rounded and flowing designs   • Softly unconstructed shapes   • Raglan or softly set-in shoulders; not very square   • Easy movement in skirts

Fabrics

• Jersey (cotton, wool, silk, blend)   • Silk crêpe de Chine   • Silk-like micro-fibres   • Stone-washed silk   • Wool crêpe   • Fine flannel • Bouclé   • Lambswool   • Chambray   • Soft brocades

Details

• Draped collars, such as shawl collars   • Lapel-less jackets   • Soft necklines   • Cinched waists; belted designs   • Soft gathers, inverted pleats at waistline   • Gored, bell, sarong, dirndl skirts

Patterns

• Paisleys   • Soft abstracts   • Polka dots   • Multi-coloured weaves (not square)   • Abstract florals (flowers generally aren't professional)

Softened straight figure

THE SOFTENED STRAIGHT WOMAN'S CLOTHES OPTIONS

Many women are a combination of angles and curves; in CMB parlance they are a **Soft Straight** type. These women have very straight shoulders but a definite waist and a curvy bottom. They need to follow some of the advice for the **Angular** women in silhouettes and details but use the softer fabrics recommended for the **Curvy** women. They don't need the same amount of softness as the **Curvy** women, nor the really crisp look so wonderful on **Angular** women. If you are a **Soft Straight** woman, it is really over the waist and bottom that you want the ease and movement, so wear the same skirts and trousers as your **Curvy** friends.

THE FULL-FIGURED, ROUND-BODIED WOMAN'S CLOTHES OPTIONS

This figure can look wonderful at work or at play. She just has to be very selective in putting her look together. If this is your body shape, you are probably fullest in the waist (often this problem is exacerbated by you being shorter in the waist, but you may have terrific long legs!). You need simple styles that drape from the shoulder in a straight line, distracting the eye away from your fullest point, the waist. So, follow the advice of the Angular women but use fabrics that move (e.g. those advised for Curvy women).

BALANCING TRICKS

Now let's look in more detail at very common figure problems. The key to a terrific look, whatever your body shape, is to be in harmony with yourself and to aim for a balanced look. When hemlines soar above the knee or drop dramatically to the ankles, getting this balanced look can be tricky for those of us who are not perfectly proportioned, but look upon this as an interesting challenge, not an impossible hurdle.

Here are a few of the most frequent challenges, with suggestions for creating an illusion of a proportioned or balanced figure.

Full figure

PEAR-SHAPES

If you are narrow at the shoulders, never buy a jacket that is neat and fitted. Your goal is to look wider in the shoulders and the way to achieve this is to wear loose jackets and tops and to layer your look above the waist. So, if you are a size 18 in skirts and trousers and size 14 on top, try on a size 16 jacket. Have the sleeves shortened, if necessary, and have the collar altered to fit more snugly if possible. Minimise the volume on your lower half within the limits of comfort: avoid wide skirts or those cut on the bias, which would visually 'pull you down' and create more 'weight' on your bottom half (where you don't want it).

Wear brighter colours, patterns and details on your top half. Try layering with shawls or scarves; or wear a waistcoat underneath your jacket to add needed volume.

SHORT-WAISTS

Women with this figure problem can be very trim and yet look fat, if they choose the wrong style jacket or dress.

Longer jackets (below the hip-line to just above the knee) are more flattering because they draw attention away from where you have no length. Team the jackets with short or long skirts. You are better in the latter, as you probably have been overcompensated with long legs and can therefore successfully show-off the more interesting, longer lengths.

59

Just avoid full skirts. Long, and lean styles are more professional.

A trick that brings 'wow-wees' from my audiences, is that if you wear a belt in the same colour as your top or blouse you can actually add length to your short torso. This is particularly effective when wearing black, navy or other neutral colours but I would not recommend you to wear white belts with your white blouses. So this tip, while effective, has its limits.

In dresses, opt for the simple coatdress, chemise or dropped waistline to look your sleekest.

LONG-WAISTS

If this is your particular challenge, you'd probably describe yourself as being 'all body and no legs'. To create balance you need to make your lower half appear longer and to shorten your long torso. The short jacket was made for you. Long styles squash you deeper into the ground unless worn with a short skirt just peaking out from underneath. Keep the attention at the waist – which is often enviably trim on women of this type – and above, with minimal details in your skirts and trousers.

Emphasise your waist by using belts to 'break-up' the area visually, but avoid belts in the same colour as your top because these would only serve to make you look even longer through the waist. If you match your belts to your skirts and trousers instead, you will elongate the lower half.

Show some leg, too. Even when longer styles prevail, wear your skirts no lower than mid-calf. Your best skirt length, if your legs are good, will be at or above the knee.

When buying dresses, try waisted designs, empire or a chemise style to which you can add a really interesting belt.

For more details on successfully handling your particular figure challenges see *The Complete Style Guide*.

ABOVE OR BELOW AVERAGE SIZE

Women who are not *average* in size can have enormous challenges in finding clothes to look good at work. America is heaven for these 'out-sizes', with stores at every price point catering for women of all shapes and sizes. Outside the States, the average-sized woman is determined by each country's fashion industry. She and her lucky friends a few sizes smaller or larger are the ones with the most choice. In Germany, tall women do very well, while the petite ones and those of average height but overweight have difficulty. In France, every woman is expected to have small bones and be average to short; so the tall and the heavy have nowhere to shop. In Britain, where almost 50 per cent of the population are over a size 16 and under 5ft 4 inches, the industry surprisingly caters for an 'average' woman two sizes smaller and two inches taller, so most British women have difficulty in getting things that fit properly.

With fashions for larger and smaller women being harder to find, here are some extra tips for those who are not 'Ms Average', but who need to – and **can** – look successful.

LARGE WOMEN

You can't afford to settle for clothes that 'make do'. With the prevailing prejudice against those who are overweight, you need to do everything you can to look healthy, energetic and professional.

Wearing the colours from your seasonal palette can help on all counts. Check again in the previous chapter, and see if your own wardrobe contains the shades that bring out the best in you, that focus attention to your face. Be bold in your colour choices for blouses, jackets and scarves, and opt for neutral and deeper tones for skirts and trousers.

Simplicity in style is most effective for you. Avoid distinguishable patterns in suits (jackets, skirts and blouses), choosing plain, quality fabrics in your best colours. Attractive patterns should be reserved for your blouses or scarves. Use striking accessories like brooches, earrings or a printed shawl draped over one shoulder.

Keep the cut of your clothes loose and elegant. Store away any blouses, jackets and skirts with straining buttons or fastenings until you are that size again or, if you are happy with your present size, regardless of dimensions, let others know it by wearing attractive outfits to project confidence in who you are. Resolve to sell quality garments that no longer fit to one of the many 'thrift' shops now opening up on local high streets. Failing that, give them away to a smaller friend, or a charity shop.

See the guidelines on proper fit in Chapter 7. All apply to you, as they do for the averaged size women. The colour, quality and fit of your clothes are more important than the style. Hence, worry less about being at the cutting edge of fashion and concentrate instead on looking appropriate, elegant and timeless.

If rethinking your size, and possibly considering a diet and exercise programme, in the meantime look your best every day by paying extra attention to your grooming. Treat yourself to a new hairstyle or hair colour (only going so far as to enhance what is or was natural) and wear perfect make-up every day. Your colleagues and clients will be so dazzled by your face that they won't 'size you up'. The following guidelines on clothes to try, or avoid, should also help.

What to try	What to avoid
Easy jackets and tops that end below your widest point, e.g. under your bottom or longer.	Any waist definition, such as found on fitted jackets and dresses.
Unconstructed jackets like the 'cardigan' style jacket.	Patterns on your lower half.
Tunic tops, loose waistcoats, or smart overblouses in substantial, not flimsy, fabric in lieu of jackets.	Bulky texture. 'Fat fabrics' such as mohair, loose knit, heavy tweeds will make you look fuller.
Solid dark colours on your lower half. Your brightest 'personality' colours near your face.	Light colours except in blouses.
Vertical patterns, e.g. pin-stripes.	Horizontal patterns or defining features.
Bold patterns in blouses and scarves.	Dinky, 'twee' patterns.
Loose-fitting clothes.	Anything too snug.
Long jewellery to create vertical lines.	Chokers and short necklaces define the width of your neck, which you might not want.
Bold accessories balance best with your size.	Tiny accessories make you look larger.
Darker toned hosiery.	Light or 'suntan' hosiery.
Substantial shoes with a modest, stacked heel are best, e.g. the classic court.	Flat shoes or stilettos.

SMALL WOMEN

Petite women in business can have a hard time establishing a presence due to their small stature. They might be human dynamos but can give the opposite impression if they dress in a way that emphasises both their sex and diminutive stature.

Through colour, you can project presence and strength. Use the deepest and the boldest colours in your seasonal palette, regardless of your personality, to look more substantial and positive. Sweet pastels project vulnerability and will ensure you get passed over every time you wear them. Neutral colours in small but 'business-like' patterns, such as pinstripes, houndstooth, Prince of Wales checks, are preferable to florals or anything too feminine. Using one colour or monochromatic blends of one colour (for example, toning shades of blue) can help to create an illusion of greater height.

Show your legs! Long skirts, no matter how chic, current and comfortable, simply swamp you. Trousers suits often work well on petite women projecting a 'pseudo-macho' confidence without really threatening the boys. How can you at 5ft 2inches?

Avoid twinky accessories and details, such as lace or bow collars, antique dangling earrings or tiny, insignificant brooches. You do have to be careful not to appear that you are being worn by your accessories rather than vice versa – they must be in scale – but they must also be significant.

A modest heel will enhance your natural stature but don't ever try to fake extra inches – because you won't succeed – in stilettos; small women tottering along in ridiculously high heels are a comical sight. You can't make a strong entrance in such styles and you risk making a complete fool of yourself if you fall in them.

What to try	What to avoid
Fitted jackets, if complimentary.	Loose, overscale jackets which will swamp you.
Finely-woven, 'tight' fabrics.	A lot of bulk and texture.
If thin, layer loose-fitted components; for example, a blouse, waistcoat then a jacket.	Excessive shoulder pads.
Modest patterns.	Very bold or contrasting patterns can overwhelm your small stature.
High confidence colours in jackets, suits and dresses – your red, blues, purples, etc.	Very light or very dark colours, head to toe.

PROPORTIONAL DRESSING

1. Suit components in equal proportions divide the body in half. On petites, best only if in the same colour. Avoid if big-boned

2. Short or cropped jackets with trousers give illusion of longer legs. Good for petites and average as well as long-waisted. Trim bottoms and thighs necessary

3. Longer jackets lengthen the torso. Good on the average to tall and short or full-waisted

4. Long jackets with long skirts are only for the over 5' 7" and the long-legged. Petites avoid at all cost

5. Here's how petite to average women look sharpest in the long-skirted suit (unless short-waisted)

6. Longer jackets are most comfortable for all sizes. For petite to average, have jackets almost reach skirt hem. Good on shorter women with full figures. Single-breasted designs are the most slimming

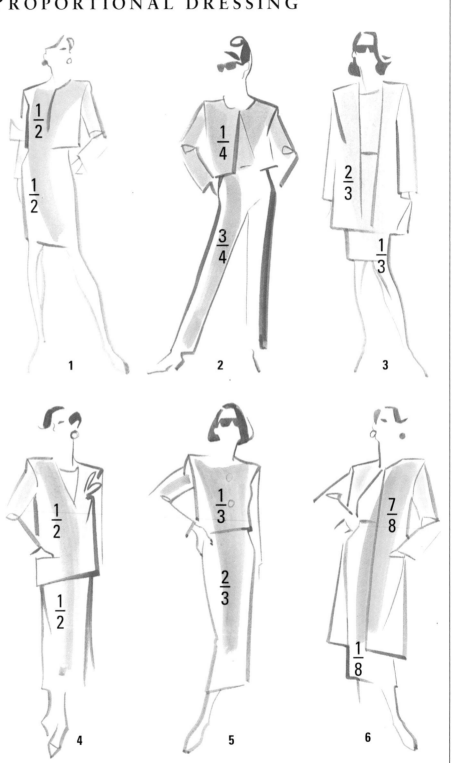

CHAPTER 6

A Wardrobe that Works

Back to the wardrobe. Have you already taken the time to develop a colour co-ordinated theme, grouping your present wardrobe of jackets, skirts, blouses and trousers together, according to colour compatibility to help bring reason and greater versatility to your life? If not, then start today.

So far, we've talked about the colours and styles that will be most flattering to you. Now we need to identify a number of basic garments that in various permutations will give you the most variety for your busy life, bearing in mind your seasonal palette wardrobe options, and the fabrics, textures and styles appropriate for your body type. With any luck, you may have some, if not all, of these in your present wardrobe – in which case you can move on to the suggestions for gradually building up that basic components wardrobe into an even more versatile one.

BUILDING A WORKING WARDROBE

Let's take various wardrobe components and consider how they could co-ordinate to create countless different options, enabling you to look wonderful every day and get the most mileage out of your clothing investments. The following sections show possibilities for the four different body types discussed in the previous chapter. For your shape, there will be 10 basic pieces that will flatter your figure and mix and match with ease. These 10 basics can create at least 15 outfits, enough for you to look different every day for 3 weeks. Select a colour combination from your palette in Chapter 4 then see what items you already have in your existing wardrobe that can fit into the scheme. For items you are missing, draw up a Shopping Priority List and start saving for these key investments.

THE ANGULAR WOMAN'S WORKING WARDROBE

(The colour scheme shown here would suit a woman who has Warm Autumn colouring.)
1. A double-breasted jacket with matching trousers (number 5)   **2.** Blouse   **3.** A single-breasted jacket worn with matching skirt (number 4)   **4.** Pleated skirt (short)   **5.** Trousers
6. Fine-ribbed polo   **7.** A short jacket   **8.** A slim skirt (long with vent or kick-pleat)
9. Dress   **10.** Patterned T-shirt

How they work together
3 + 4, add a necklace or scarf for interest; 3 + 5 + 6, add a brooch; 1 + 2 + 4; 1 + 5 + 10;
1 + 6 + 8; 3 + 4 + 10; 6 + 7 + 8; 1 + 5 + 6; 7 + 9; 9, add a scarf; 7 + 2 + 5; 6 + 4 +7;
3 + 8; 3 + 9; 7 + 2 + 5.

THE CURVY WOMAN'S WORKING WARDROBE

(The colour scheme shown here would look wonderful on a woman who is Soft in colouring.)
1. Soft jacket worn with matching skirt (number 8)   **2.** Blouse   **3.** Jacket   **4.** Soft-fitted, short skirt   **5.** Fluid trousers   **6.** Jersey top   **7.** Fitted jacket   **8.** Long, gored skirt
9. Softly-fitted dress   **10.** Silk T-shirt

How they work together
3 + 4 + 10; 2 + 7 + 5; 1 + 2 + 8; 3 + 8 + 10; 1 + 2 + 5; 7 + 10 + 4; 3 + 6 + 5 (add a necklace); 7 + 2 + 8; 7 + 9; 6 + 1 + 5; 7 + 8 +10; 7 + 10 + 5; 6 + 1 + 8; 3 + 9; 3 + 2 + 5.

THE SOFTENED STRAIGHT WOMAN'S WORKING WARDROBE

(The colour scheme shown here would complement a woman with Deep or clear colouring.)

1. Soft jacket worn with matching skirt (number 8)   **2.** Blouse   **3.** Collarless jacket
4. Pleated skirt   **5.** Trousers   **6.** Body suit   **7.** Double-breasted jacket   **8.** Long skirt
9. Dress   **10.** Jersey top

How they work together

3 + 6 + 4; 1 + 2 + 5; 7 + 10 + 4; 1 + 2 + 4; 3 + 9 (add a necklace); 1 + 6 + 5; 7 + 10 + 8;
2 + 3 + 8; 3 + 6 +5; 7 + 9; 9 + 1; 2 + 5 + 1; 8 + 2 + 3; 1 + 6 + 8; 7 + 6 + 5.

THE FULL-FIGURED WOMAN'S WORKING WARDROBE

(The colour scheme of this wardrobe would be perfect for a woman who has Cool colouring.)
1. Long, collarless jacket   2. Soft, cross-over blouse   3. Long, pleated skirt (elasticated waist)   4. Mid-calf culottes   5. Cardigan jacket   6. Long fluid trousers
7. Long-sleeve T-shirt (silk)   8. Elasticated straight skirt (just below knee)
9. Patterned, long, silk blouse   10. Swing dress

How they work together
1 + 2+ 3; 1 + 9 + 4; 5 + 2 + 8; 1 + 7 + 6; 10 + 5; 9 + 4; 1 + 7 + 9 + 6;
9 + 8; 5 + 9 + 3; 5 + 9 + 4; 1 + 2 +8; 4 + 1 + 7; 10 + 1; 6 + 9 + 5;
1 + 2 + 6.

VERSATILE INVESTMENTS

Few of us can afford to clear out our existing wardrobe, so let's think about what you already have in your collection, and see if you have suits and outfits that are fulfilling all your needs.

THE STRONG NEUTRAL SUIT

Every woman needs a suit that sets the stage for her to be taken seriously. There will be occasions when you feel underconfident, or need to project your professionalism to an audience who may not yet value your contribution. And there will be times when you need to let folks know who's in-charge, that is, *YOU!!*

Hence, this suit is all about gravitas. Choose the most sober, deep neutral that you can wear without looking too boring, severe or washed-out. Charcoal, navy, olive, a rich burgundy, plum or mahogany are all good possibilities.

This suit will look strongest, yet conservative, if worn as a matching set. When you want to soften the look, try contrasting, toning or patterned skirts.

To play safest and to project the most authority, team it with a blouse in your white (soft, pure or ivory). However, a pastel blouse with just a hint of colour will be more feminine and probably more flattering. On occasions when you don't need to be at the helm, you can brighten-up the look with more colourful blouses and prints.

Choose a jacket design that will accommodate many different necklines. One without lapels would set off blouses with high collars, and could either have a simple jewel or V-neckline – also allowing you to tuck pretty printed scarves inside for variety.

This power suit will look most strong if teamed with a confident brooch and smart earrings.

THE LIGHT NEUTRAL SUIT

For spring and summer wear, you will need suits that are as versatile as your navy, olive, burgundy and charcoal ones but lighter, and more welcoming while still looking professional. Increasingly now, we are offered wonderful multi-purpose colours, such as ivory, stone, taupe, pewter, camel and cocoa brown.

Any woman, regardless of her colouring, can wear stone or taupe provided that she balances it with a terrific colour from her palette. For example, Deep and Clear women might wear taupe with black, red, purple or royal blue. Light and Cool women might try rose pink, soft fuchsia or lavender. Warm and Soft women can wear rust, moss green or turquoise with stone.

The lighter the suit, the better the quality required. You can cheat with navies, blacks and greys but rarely with a light colour. Be honest about the likelihood of being able to keep the suit clean. If you commute to work on public transport, ivory probably is a silly choice no matter how terrific it looks on you.

Thinking of ivory, there is a huge difference between ivory and white. The former is elegant and the latter rarely so, even if you work in a warm, sunny climate. An ivory jacket is particularly useful, as it will go with everything – plains as well as many weaves.

THE COLOURED SUIT

In the last decade, certain colours have become so widespread for business women's wear that they are accepted as neutral options. A red suit should feature in every working woman's wardrobe (or, at least, a red jacket to team with your skirts). Red tells colleagues, managers and customers alike that you know who you are, and are prepared to stand your ground. Wear red to the next large meeting or conference you attend and see how more people come up to you and introduce themselves. In grey, you can attend functions and blend into the woodwork if that is what you wish. In red, people think you must have something to say – so be prepared to speak your piece!

Another great new neutral is purple, which comes in deep rich shades as well as softer, violet versions. Choose one that is neither too delicate (such as pale lavender) nor too electric (usually with really garish buttons). Again, any woman can wear purple. If you are a Deep and Clear woman, offset it with red, black or mango. If Light, Soft and Cool go monochromatic, teaming it with softer lilac or rose. If you have Warm colouring, try mustard or gold with purple – it'll be a knockout on you.

The red or purple jacket of your suit will work with many other basic colours, both light and dark, in your wardrobe. And both are wonderful with black or grey trousers, which the most confident women already know.

THE TROUSER/CULOTTE SUIT

The time has come for all women who know trousers or culottes are flattering on them (and want to wear them), to brave the workplace in these comfortable alternatives to the skirted suit.

As with a light coloured suit, you can't cheat on quality when buying trousers or culottes, so don't gamble away your chances of carrying off this sometimes risky look with any old pair of trousers teamed with any old jacket.

For guidance on selecting the best trouser and culotte styles, see Chapter 7.

THE DAY-TO-EVENING ENSEMBLE

There will be occasions when your working day does not end when the office closes but continues over dinner with colleagues or clients. Unlike men, few women socialise on business for the fun of it and aim to achieve positive results. After all, men can look totally acceptable in the same, smart, neutral suit they've worn all day, but we women have to make more effort if we're to avoid what CMB consultants call the 'left-over office' look ... the basic suit, cotton blouse, evaporated make-up, daytime accessories, etc.

If an evening event is planned, dress in the morning in something that is 'transformable' at 5 p.m. Bring along one of those wonderful, uncrushable georgette pleated skirts in a long length to make your day-time suit jacket look completely different. Wear a blouse with a slight sheen, that will pick up the light.

Change your basic leather belt for one with beading, fake jewels or a gold trim. Add extra gold and/or pearl ropes. Replace your button ear-

below Day: Start the day with basics which only require minor adjustments to work in the evening

centre Evening: For a working dinner, a change of top, from a woollen to lace body suit, is simple and effective. Coloured stone, diamanté or dangling earrings will help you sparkle outside the office. Remember to enhance your make-up with deeper or brighter colours for evening

right An evening with friends: Discard the jacket and skirt and add a fun waistcoat and trousers to put you in style for a night on the town

rings with a pair that dangle. Touch up your make-up – completely, not just some powder and lipstick. Finally, add a nice scent – it will make you feel special and put you in the right mood for a social, albeit still business, evening.

DRESS ALTERNATIVES

If you haven't discovered the ease and comfort of wearing simple dresses in lieu of skirts and blouses under jackets or on their own, then now is the time to do so. For women of every shape and size there are terrific options in basic plain colours as well as patterns.

Dresses are for days you don't need to look 'in-charge'. They are terrific for staff meetings, for working with colleagues, and for brainstorming sessions.

The simpler the design of the dress, the more you can change its look by adding a belt or scarf, wearing a brooch or chains, co-ordinating with different jacket lengths and styles.

Choose the fabric carefully. Many are too flimsy and clingy for the office (especially some knits, jerseys and silks). To look smart and appropriate at work, it is best if the dress is completely lined. For advice on getting a nice fit, see Chapter 7.

OVERCOATS AND RAINCOATS

Your investment in a coat will be a major one which can put other purchases on hold for many months, so you must think and plan what you need and want before you even enter a store to buy one.

When skirt hemlines start fluctuating you can have real problems selecting a coat that will work with everything . . . but it must. So decide what hemline is best for you and get a coat that accommodates that particular length. Nothing looks more shabby than a coat that is too short for a skirt or dress, although a long coat over a shorter skirt is quite acceptable.

Once the coat length is settled, consider the desired weight. If you travel by public transport you need more warmth – such as a wool or wool and cashmere blend will provide – than if you travel by car. If you are a walker you will need a coat that is lightweight but still warm and capable of protecting you from the unpredicted shower. Some microfibres will suit your needs best.

When it comes to colour, splash out! You don't need to stick to a safe neutral such as black, tan or navy. Cheer yourself and everyone you meet with a lovely shade that will brighten up the dull mid-winter landscape, but be smart and opt for mid to deep shades rather than light ones that require regular cleaning.

A macintosh or raincoat might be a more versatile investment than a woollen coat, particularly if you live in an inclement climate. Today you can find dashing yet totally serviceable, wet-proof designs to see you through the worst weather.

Always try coats on when you are wearing a suit jacket underneath – and still allow room for layering if necessary. For example, if you decide to invest in one terrific raincoat it should be roomy enough also to accommodate an extra sweater, even under your suit jacket, if needed in mid-winter to keep you warm.

Over the years develop a coat wardrobe of varying lengths, weights and colours, to see you through rain and shine in style. Check your coats regularly to see that they look their best. Replace lost buttons, be sure the hem is even and repair any fraying, even inside . . . this can occur, for example, at the armpits, which take great strain if the coat *is* a bit snug.

If you have a coat that is still wearable but you find it boring, consider the following ideas for giving it, and you, a new look.

- ◆ Change the buttons for bright new ones of good quality gilt, bone, or a contrasting colour

- ◆ Add a colourful shawl or scarf from your collection, to make it look different every day

- ◆ If it is a belted style, use a leather belt rather than the one that came with the coat

- ◆ Wear a large, attractive brooch

- ◆ Draw attention from the coat by wearing with it a terrific fedora, beret or floppy felt hat

S UMMER MADNESS

Something strange happens as soon as the sun begins to shine, signalling the beginning of summer. Sane women can lose their professional sensibilities and reveal a different image from the one they have projected for the major part of the year. This transformation is often most pronounced in northern climates with brief summers. In others, with reasonably moderate to warm weather for many months or all year round, this delirium doesn't seem to set in in the way it does in countries like Britain, Germany and Scandinavia.

left: Dressed to kill your career prospects: Floral sun-dresses, white shoes and bare legs scream 'unprofessional', whatever the weather

right: Keeping cool and keeping the professional edge: Short-sleeve cotton jackets teamed with light-weight skirts, in business colours, present the right image in summer

A warm day seems to signal a licence to strip off the essential layers of a woman's 'business armour'. Off come the tights, on go sandals, open-toed shoes or, even worse, *white* shoes! These first signs of 'summer madness' are followed by bare arms, low cut blouses and sundresses under jackets which are discarded at some point during the day, leaving the owners looking not only unprofessional but vulnerable. The smart tailored looks worn religiously throughout the rest of the year are shelved in preference for crease-prone linen, see-through blouses, rising hemlines, shorts, tank-tops, T-shirts. The damage many women do to their image in just these two or three short months every summer damages their prospects throughout the remainder of the year.

Male colleagues don't know what to say, how to react or where to look when this summer madness starts. My business booms every summer; I receive dozens of calls from personnel officers asking if a consultant could please come in to discuss image with the women, and would we please tell them not to wear sundresses and sandals to the office. These calls come from the large multi-nationals as well as the small companies.

My advice is that as soon as it gets hot, try to stay cool, in every sense of the word. Do not read the women's magazines for advice on what fun you can have, in looking great yet keeping cool. The girls who are doling it out work in a highly creative, informal environment where they have the freedom to wear halter tops, denim mini-skirts and Lycra dresses to the office. But you work in the real world, where you need to take your image seriously all year round. Because if *you* don't, why should anyone else?

If you live in a climate that is sunny and warm for a good portion of the year, no doubt your business world hardly notices any transition in image. Your clothes are doubtless lighter both in fabric and colour, but your offices are air-conditioned, which makes the wearing of hosiery expected and comfortable. However, in countries with very brief periods of warm weather, many offices do not have air-conditioning and can become quite unbearably hot. This is what leads to such bizarre dress. But the men don't react to the discomfort by dressing in shorts and T-shirts. So why do women?

BEST BETS FOR KEEPING AND LOOKING COOL

In the summertime, remember that you need to maintain the same professional standards that you displayed during the rest of the year. This can easily be achieved if you buy the same garments but in light fabrics. I know this may sound all too obvious, but it bears repeating as many women really do think that the summertime grants them liberties to wear garments designed as leisure-wear.

A lightweight suit, a dress and jacket, or a blouse, jacket and matching or co-ordinating skirt or trousers are more appropriate. Dresses that are 'substantial' in their own right, that is, a coat dress, shirtwaister or chemise in a medium weight, not a clingy or sheer, fabric are acceptable on their own when you are working at your desk. But remember, for any meeting, you need to attend wearing a jacket and discard this only when your superiors do so, or you are invited to do so if you wish.

Choose fabrics with very high percentage of natural fibres, but containing a minimal blend of a man-made material such as micro-fibres, rayon, polyester or nylon which helps prevent wrinkling and are machine- or hand-washable. Blouses and dresses in natural fabrics such as cotton, linen, silk and cool wool can usually be worn only once in warm weather. Check also to see whether the care label stresses dry-cleaning only because this is not only expensive but impractical for women who travel extensively.

Wear low-denier hosiery at all times on business. Number 5, 7, or 10 denier are very comfortable in tights, even more so in stockings or hold-ups which allow more ventilation. There is a very wide range of soft neutral shades available now, and it is an easy matter to find appropriate ones to tone in with your outfit – taupe, pale beige, soft ivory, slate-grey, and so on.

Select blouses with, at minimum, a short or capped sleeve; never wear sleeveless ones in the office unless you keep your jacket on all day. No matter how trim and well-toned your arms may be, bare armpits do little to project professionalism. Again, the men don't get away with it, so why should you?

In shoes and accessories, choose comparable styles and quality to those you wear during the rest of the year, but in lighter colours. Taupe, pewter and light grey are a welcome relief from the dark navy, black and brown worn so often in winter. Also, coloured shoes to tone with outfits are more acceptable in the summertime than in winter; for example, blue, red or purple. The only colour that 'shoots you in the foot' is *white*. At any price, by any designer, white shoes are tacky and incapable of projecting success.

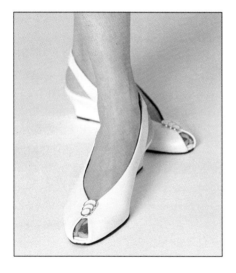

White shoes have no place in business. Never expose your tootsies, no matter how nice the pedicure. Sling backs are acceptable, open-toes are not

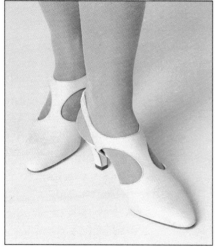

Ivory, taupe or stone-coloured shoes are fine for summertime. But with dark coloured skirts and dresses always wear a darker shoe. Light denier hosiery is a must no matter what the temperature

CHAPTER 7

Getting the Style and Fit Right

Your working wardrobe needs to be planned for, and bought, in a completely different frame of mind from when you are buying weekend or party gear. What you consider to be a good style or fit when selecting leisure clothes is most likely to be completely wrong for the office.

We've already looked at style issues in Chapters 5 and 6, and there's more advice here, but first let me concentrate on fit, because it is crucial that you get it right. The fit of your clothes can make or break your overall business image. If they are too big or loose, you will look as if you either borrowed them or have lost weight (too much). If your clothes fit too snugly, your body becomes the focus of everyone's attention, either because you simply look overweight or, because your clothes are too figure-hugging, that is, provocative. You might attract the interest of male colleagues, but they won't be concentrating on your business acumen because you will be sending out mixed messages!

So, fit is very important. Forget what size you are. Size is irrelevant and manufacturers are so inconsistent that you are smarter to shop thinking of getting the look right. Remember, people don't have x-ray vision and can't read the labels inside your clothes to see the size! If the very thought bothers you, you can always snip the size label out anyway, once the garment is yours.

A fit that allows you to move easily, as well as add a few extra pounds during the month, is what you should aim for in all your wardrobe items. Slightly loose – not baggy – clothes are more elegant and slimming than tighter-fitting ones and significantly more comfortable for 10 to 12 hours of continuous wear.

Now let's look at individual garments and the style and fit points to bear in mind when you are buying them.

SKIRTS

Your objective will be to wear styles and sizes that are comfortable and require no fuss to keep in place. You know those straight skirts that look so great when you try them on but as soon as you sit down require constant tugging to keep them from riding up your thighs. A skirt can rise slightly, provided it didn't start out too short, when you sit but you shouldn't need to be consciously worrying about it all the time. If you are, it is probably too short or too tight.

Be honest about your side view in skirts. If your tummy and bottom are curvy, a skirt without darts is unforgiving and looks unattractive. You will look chubby even if you aren't. If you retain fluid during the month, try shopping then, to be sure that you get a fit that is bearable on those regular days when you need extra space.

If you notice horizontal lines ('stretchmarks') across the front of your skirts then the fit is wrong. Waistbands that curl over when you are seated look terrible. Hide any you might have presently under a belt and next time you shop for a skirt choose a different waist, i.e. one with softer gathers and a better fit. If the problem is caused by the fact that you are short-waisted, look for a skirt without a waistband, or a very narrow one.

Length is a matter of taste, fashion and proportions. Fortunately, the fluctuations are less frequent in fashion today and women do have a choice so consider first and foremost what is flattering on you. If your legs aren't an asset, minimise attention there by wearing longer, easy hemlines toned-in with matching hosiery. If you are short but also have unattractive legs you know you need to show more leg just to look balanced. Try a hem just below the knee, where your leg naturally indents, and finish with deeper (but not opaque), toning hosiery. Tulip- or bell-

left Skirts that strain are a pain . . . they look and feel awful

centre Wearing tight skirts only asks for trouble in business

right Aim for elegance in the fit of your skirts. You'll look slimmer and more professional if you do

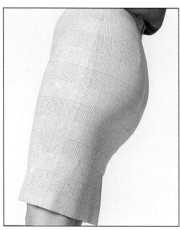

shaped skirts are more flattering and slimming than straight, boxy styles. A-line skirts make all women look shorter and wider.

Taller women look great in longer lengths but need to be careful when it comes to volume. Wide, full skirts don't look professional no matter how flattering or fashionable. If you like them long be sure the balance is right; that is, that all the attention isn't drawn to below your waist.

When considering a longer length skirt for work, always walk around the fashion floor of the store wearing it, to see what happens when you move and whether it will be manageable through your daily obstacle course. Some styles allow very little movement and you'll find yourself limited to taking 'baby steps' all day. Other longer styles can twist around or creep up your legs.

Very full, long skirts are too 'social' and relaxed for the office. It's near impossible to look commanding in a full, swirling skirt. If you love long, easy skirts for their comfort as well as their style, try ones cut on the bias, which will give you the movement without the volume.

JACKETS

The easiest way to wreck your look is to wear cheap and/or ill-fitted jackets.

When shopping, wear a blouse that you would be likely to wear under the jacket. If this isn't practicable, select an appropriate blouse in the shop before trying on the suit. Starting at the shoulders, ask yourself if the outline or silhouette is complimentary? Droopy, shapeless shoulders don't project much strength and can look too relaxed for business. If you love the jacket aside from the shoulders, ask yourself if a pair of shoulder-

Left Don't box your feminine style into stiff, ill-fitting jackets

right Easy, looser-fitting jackets are more flattering on many women. When buttoned, they should fit loosely and drape over your body

pads would be all that's required to rescue the look. Better still, take a pair of removable pads with you, so you can quickly pop them in and see if they do the trick.

The best shoulders should look natural, never severe. Excessively-padded models, thankfully, are a thing of the past. If you like shoulder-pads to help balance your hips (they almost always make you less hippy) by all means try some modest ones. Another possibility, to create a better balance with a larger hip measurement, would be to try the jacket in a size larger, but this won't look right if the jacket is tailored. It only works with less structured styles.

For any presentation, you need to speak with the jacket buttoned, so be sure the lapels, buttons and any vents aren't straining; it needs to look smooth and comfortable when buttoned-up.

Often I see women in wonderful jackets but looking 'overwhelmed' because the sleeves are too long, or looking gawky because the sleeves are too short. As someone who always has to have sleeves shortened by several inches, I know that even a half-inch wrong either way can mar your image. If you have long arms, never buy a jacket without first checking to see that there is ample fabric to bring the sleeves down. For the short-limbed, always get the sleeves altered (before you ever wear it). And unless you are a very skilled dressmaker/tailoress, this is one of those

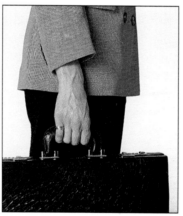

Sleeves that are too long make you look dwarfed by your jacket

Sleeves that are too short never look elegant, however costly the jacket

The correct sleeve length ends just at the break of the wrist

alterations best done by the shop or store where you make the purchase – particularly if the sleeves are fully lined. Or, invest in some expandable arm bands (sold in men's departments) which you wear above the elbow and cover with the excessive inches from the sleeves.

The correct length of the jacket will depend on your proportions. Those with balanced bodies have the choice of any length (lucky women). See illustrations on page 64 for more ideas about what might suit you best. If you are long in the body, only wear long jackets with a short skirt. Otherwise, your most attractive cut will be short, that is, never below your hip bone. For short-waisted women, your jackets are best in longer lengths.

Your bustline is an important factor when you're choosing a good-fitting jacket. If you have a full bust, the fabric should be easy, not stiff, and should fall smoothly over the bust, without sticking out or seeming to stretch. If you have an average bust, be sure not to minimise what you have in too loose-fitting jackets. Small-busted women benefit from a looser fit, and extra details such as pockets and exaggerated lapels to add bulk where it is needed.

B LOUSES

Today you have endless possibilities for blouses to wear under your suits, but I urge you to think 'simple and elegant'. By all means have fun with colour and fabric, but keep the neckline and details unfussy. Remember, you want to be able to wear it with several of the jackets in your wardrobe. Too often, elaborate designs are best worn alone, not under a jacket at all, and most are not suitable for business-wear. If in doubt when shopping for blouses, return to the shop wearing one of your suits and try the blouse on again, to see if it works.

When it comes to fabric, never wear ones that are too sheer or too snug; for example, Lycra bodysuits. I own several of these but only wear them on days I am committed to never taking my jacket off (since I am freezing most of the time, this is easily done).

left Never buy or wear a blouse that's straining across the bust

right A loose fit in your blouses is both slimming and elegant

Also, watch the neckline. A much repeated CMB caveat to working women is: 'the more you show the less authority you have.' This goes for both necklines and hemlines.

TROUSERS

I hear you thinking, 'I could never get away with trousers where I work'. Indeed, many companies actively discourage or specifically prohibit women from wearing trousers. Men, too often the bosses, have a problem with women in trousers; they simply don't know how to deal with them. But it's only a matter of time before trousers for women are considered more widely acceptable. Scandinavian and German women have a good laugh at such concerns, as trousers are widely worn by working women in these countries.

Unfortunately, women sometimes take liberties in a relaxed business environment by wearing any old trousers with a blouse or sweater. Whenever company managers seek advice from CMB on this vexed problem, rather than talk the women out of wearing trousers I try to convince companies that *trouser suits* should be allowed and the women be given guidance on how to wear them.

To even consider trousers for work, you need to be very honest about how you look in them from the front, side and rear. If you aren't an absolute winner from all three vantage points, don't wear them to work. If you are, and like the ease of a trouser suit, by all means consider one if you think you can get away with it.

Trousers that are too tight are unprofessional . . . no matter how trim your figure. Check the fit of yours from front, side and rear

left From the front you want the trousers to drape, so styles with darts or inverted pleats are best

right You should be able to get your hands in the pockets without straining the seams

The most effective suits are those in elegant neutral colours (that is, not yellow, pink or patterned) in good quality fabric. The more substantial the fabric – in weight and texture – the better.

Accessorise a trouser suit as thoughtfully as you do your skirted- suits, that is, always with a belt, and appropriate shoes. A smart shoe-boot or flats will look more relaxed, while a raised heel makes a trouser suit more dressy. Don't forget your earrings, a necklace or brooch, which give the professional stamp to any trouser suit.

NICE KNITS

Knits can feature in every working woman's wardrobe. They are easy to wear, comfortable and don't crease, and are favoured by many women who travel

Take care that your knits don't reveal too much (far left). Because they cling they can expose your curves more than other fabrics. Styles which are too tight or too short, as here, only beg harassment.

Layer your knits to create ensembles that are comfortable as well as attractive (left). Keep the fit neat but easy, without exposing your curves too obviously.

CULOTTES AND SHORTS

In the last few years City Shorts have been proffered by the fashion pundits as a nice alternative for working women in the summertime. The only problem with these 'suits' is that unless the jacket is quite long and kept on all day, the look is too casual for work. Few women look elegant in shorts, regardless of their figures, and even in the most expensive silk or linen. When shorts wrinkle, as they invariably do, it is not a pretty sight. So, don't be swayed by summer fashion features in the magazines touting these as an option. They aren't. The only exception would be if you work in a very relaxed office environment and/or live in a warm climate.

Culottes are another item men have definite opinions about; generally never very positive. Often, the stores offer stunning culottes in plain or patterned fabric teamed with smart jackets, so they are effectively a suit. The key is not to have too much volume in the culottes and for the fabric to be very good quality. Cheap culottes don't fool anyone that they are anything but cheap, whereas you may get away with an inexpensive skirt worn under a jacket.

Larger women, particularly those with heavy thighs, find culottes more flattering and comfortable than trousers and skirts. If considering this look, ask yourself: 'Can I smarten it up with accessories to look strong enough to give a presentation to a small group?' If the 'culotte look' is only good enough for behind the desk, it will be of limited use and not good enough to present the consistently successful image that you want and need.

DRESSES

In the last few years, dresses have become the welcome alternative to the skirt and blouse under a jacket. Simple shifts in beautiful colours and fabrics under an unconstructed cardigan-style jacket are both easy to wear and comfortable. Against such a simple backdrop, you can add a striking necklace or a mixture of pearls and gold chains with earrings and look terrific. The 'Dress-Suit' also takes your business day wear into the evening most successfully.

Like all other items in your wardrobe, the fit of your dresses is very important. A dress only looks elegant and businesslike if it is slightly loose, not figure-hugging. This is why you should choose fabrics of substance, such as wool, wool and cotton blends, linen, tightly-woven knits, challis, etc. for dresses you want to be able to wear without a jacket.

left A simple dress in a striking colour, with short or long sleeves, is one of your most versatile wardrobe components. Always wear with a jacket for meetings and presentations

right Discard your workday jacket and transform the simple shift dress for evening with a stunning scarf and accessories

The best style for a dress you intend to wear without a jacket is the coatdress, which is tailored to look finished all on its own. A simple chemise can also be worn alone if well accessorised, and looks even more complete with a shawl (which acts like a jacket).

With lighterweight dresses of silk, viscose, rayon or jersey, always wear a jacket; otherwise, there is simply too little fabric between you and your body not to be distracting when you are working with men. A cardigan, as opposed to a knit jacket, with a dress is not smart enough for business wear.

UNDIES

Today's undergarments provide wonderful, supportive foundations to help any figure. From control-top tights to lightweight and comfortable 'girdles', there is no reason why any woman not in prime condition can't look wonderful in her clothes. But if your bra doesn't fit or your panties are too small, however trim you are, and however expensive your clothes, you will look awful!

Have you been properly measured for your bra? Quite often, when a woman is properly measured for a bra, she discovers she has been wearing the wrong size. The difference in fit and comfort in wearing the correct size is amazing, so, if you haven't been measured recently, why not go along to the lingerie department of a good store and see if you *are* wearing the right bra.

Panties that seduce, generally create the worst 'pantylines' under skirts and trousers. You know, those sexy, silky numbers that defy gravity. For every day, you want panties that are comfortable around the leg and

Be sure your undies don't let you down. Never leave home in any doubt about what you are exposing from behind

waist, and *cover your entire bottom*. The smoother the fit the better. So when buying yours be sure to allow for possible shrinkage in the dryer.

Also, take a good look at your rear view in a triple mirror and if your buttocks are less firm than they once were, do invest in a 'girdle', at least until you can get back into shape with some spot exercises. Nothing is more unprofessional and self-destructive in the workplace than a pair of jiggling buttocks under a skirt.

Finally, if your skirts and dresses are not lined it is advisable to wear an underslip to help retain their shape and prevent the skirts clinging to your legs and riding-up when you walk. If you wear varying length skirts get one slip to serve the short hemlines and another for the longer lengths.

CHAPTER 8

Power Polish

Every little detail counts when you're assembling a power outfit, but many women practise false economy by not investing in quality accessories in keeping with their suits. Remember, a cheap or worn pair of shoes immediately devalues any outfit. Similarly, any old pair of earrings, such as the ubiquitous pearl studs that many women wear with everything, minimises the impact of a stylish new suit.

I'm the first to appreciate that for working women, time is a precious commodity and shopping can be wearisome, but if you allot the time needed to buy a new suit, isn't it worth also spending a little more on whatever is required to complete the look? When you buy a new suit, of course you should consider what you already have that will go with it. But don't rely on the safe, nondescript shoes from last winter being right for this suit this winter. Every major outfit should be thought through.

THE RIGHT ACCESSORIES

Let's think of a new suit you've just bought. It's a great colour and style and feels terrific. First, ask yourself: what blouses do you have to wear with it? What colours, plain and patterned, from your existing wardrobe work best? When you get home, have a dress rehearsal. In fact, never wear a new outfit to your place of work without this preliminary trial. Try them on together to be sure the necklines and fabrics blend. If in any doubt, don't team them. If none of your blouses do the suit justice, then decide on two or three new ones that you might need to vary its look.

What about scarves? Does the collar of the jacket lend itself to adding a scarf (best if collarless, without lapels)? Now the belt: when you take off your jacket you need a belt to finish the waistline of your skirt, even if it doesn't have belt loops. You know how incomplete a man looks in trousers that are beltless; so, too, does a woman – whether wearing trousers or a skirt. Do you have a good quality leather belt, in an appropriate colour and width for the suit? A belt should look part of the suit, not stand out as an ill-judged afterthought.

What colour tights, what denier looks most elegant with the new suit? Any old pair from your existing collection could ruin the impact. Try different shades and textures, both matt and with a slight sheen. How do they look together? Try on the best options. If none look right, invest in new ones that do.

And your shoes: is the colour right? What about the heel – is it smart, comfortable and appropriate? Is the quality comparable to that of the suit? If in doubt, always wear better.

Your jewellery – the earrings – should you add a brooch or a choker? These accessories can make the suit look even more expensive and they don't have to be real gold! Go through this process for every outfit you wear to work, throughout the year. No, it is not laborious. Once you have two or three good pairs of shoes that are current and appropriate you can wear them with everything. The same applies to your collection of belts, earrings, brooches and scarves.

Here are further guidelines for selecting the right accessories to ensure your outfits all look wonderful and to help you make the best use of the gems in your existing wardrobe and eliminate past mistakes.

JEWELLERY

In business, it is best to wear only gold, silver or pearls, or combinations of these; they are the most 'serious' and professional. Diamanté and coloured stones look inappropriate during the day (even though in fashion from time to time). Wood, acrylic, rope, ribbon, rubber and so on, have no place in business (unless you are in the fashion trade).

CMB advise women with very warm colouring – golden blonde, red, strawberry or auburn hair, and possibly freckles – to wear only gold jewellery. Women with a decidedly cool look, particularly if they have grey hair, look much more attractive and harmonious in silver jewellery. Other women can wear both gold and silver, wearing them independently or in combination for variety.

Some women complain that they can only wear real gold (14c, 18c or 22c) or sterling silver, because costume jewellery brings them out in rashes. Indeed, if you can afford the real thing, wear it. For those on more limited budgets but also for those who like the variety and currentness of today's wonderful costume jewellery you can do a few things to help yourself become more tolerant.

Some women can't tolerate metal against their skin because they have a very acidic system which creates a chemical reaction against anything but pure gold or silver. If this is your problem, you can help to balance your system by avoiding very acidic foods like citrus fruit, tomatoes, wine (especially red), and eating more alkaline foods. My Ayurvedic doctor recommends eating three to four meals weekly of pears (just pears) which are highly alkaline to help balance the high acidity in your system. It works for me and has also done wonders for hundreds of my clients who love costume jewellery. Give it a try. But if it does work for you, don't be carried away by your enthusiasm. Keep the 'fun' pieces of jewellery for leisurewear.

Earrings

Another CMB adage for you: 'Earrings are equivalent in importance for a woman as a tie is for a man.' Wear them every day, for every business occasion, not just the social ones.

What to select depends on your personality, your face shape, bone structure, colouring, and the look you want to achieve/project. Never copy the style choices of a friend or colleague, however good they may look. They might look terrible on you! Always be sure you feel comfortable with the style and that it is right for you.

Next, be sure the shape is complimentary to your face. If you have a very narrow jaw line, a fuller, rounder earring is good. Broad or square-jawed women look best in flatter and longer earrings. The earrings can be bold but should not overpower your face. You want your eyes to be the centre of communication, not your earlobes. If you are petite, with a small frame, delicate designs are more in balance, while bigger-boned, larger women need more significant sizes and shapes.

Necklaces

A choker, necklace or string of pearls can complete a neckline more effectively than a fussy scarf or collar. The right style mainly depends on the length and thickness of your neck, and your bone structure.

Women with average to long necks can look wonderful in chunky chokers, and these are especially effective on a collarless jacket. If you have a short neck, this style is best avoided because it will accentuate the shortness and you will look cluttered, and possibly uncomfortable. Choose instead long, single or multi-strands of gold chains or pearls, which will create a vertical illusion and make your neck look longer.

Tall and large women look best in long ropes and can add or subtract in number within the limits of their personalities and the acceptability of such jewellery by their industry. Smaller-boned and petite women are advised to wear opera length (about 4 or 5 inches down from the collarbone); longer chains often overwhelm them. A simple long strand of pearls or a single long chain and pendant are other options for them.

A thick neck will look more slender if you wear long chains and strands, which give an elongating illusion. Thin necks, conversely, are better in shorter necklaces (including chokers that aren't too chunky), because these give volume where it is needed.

Brooches and pins

Brooches and pins are accessories to express your personality and position, so by all means be individual, just make sure the quality is up to par with the rest of your image and that the item is neither too pretty, nor too bold. If in doubt, opt for simplicity, and wear an interesting abstract shape, a stick pin or a gold and pearl brooch.

Avoid always wearing matching earrings and brooches which project a women who is not self-confident enough to put things together herself. If you love the earrings and the brooch offered in a set, by all means buy them, but wear the pieces separately from time to time.

Bracelets

Keep them to a minimum. Women who have tried striking cuffs and bangles on their writing wrist know what a bother bracelets can be. If they make a noise or thump when you write, they are a distraction. If you like to wear something more than your watch try a single or a few simple ones together with your watch for interest. Be careful that the metal or design doesn't scratch the glass facing of your watch.

WATCHES

The most significant investment, in terms of accessories, has to be your watch. Not only are women aware of each others' watches but so are men; perhaps, more so.

Today, elegant, simple and reliable watches are offered at every price. There is no reason why yours shouldn't look smart and successful even on an entry level salary. Women who don't wear watches project to others that they don't have the foggiest notion what time management means and also are probably lowly 'internal' people who never get out and about in business. How could you ever be on time for anything outside the office without a watch!

Choose a watch that is in proportion to the size of your wrist. If your watch is too small, it will look insignificant and make you look pudgy. If too heavy and/or big, you will look as if you are being worn by your watch.

Keep the face simple but with markings that you can actually read. Digitalised models, efficient and high-tech though they might be, aren't as elegant or attractive as simple, more traditional designs. Avoid ones with timers, beepers, or multi-monitors.

The higher you fly in business the more important your watch becomes, so as soon as you can afford it, get a really good one that tells everyone you are successful. But don't go overboard on styling. Choose a slim-line, classic shape in a size appropriate to your size. Petite woman should not wear man-sized watches.

PENS

A polished professional always uses a good pen, preferably a fountain pen, especially for 'topping and tailing' letters. If you prefer to draft a report with a smooth or fast disposable ballpoint, use the biro in your own office but use a smart pen for meetings or whenever you are taking notes or signing papers in front of others.

You don't need a solid gold pen to look successful. Choose a colour, weight and design that co-ordinates with the rest of your look and is comfortable to handle.

BELTS

Today we have an array of wonderful colours and textures to select from when buying belts and many look much more expensive than they actually are. Having determined the width that is comfortable on you and flatters your body type, look for the best neutral colour to work with most of your outfits. The safest choice is to match your shoes. So, if you have mainly black shoes, get a wonderful black leather belt (and a suede one for winter). Or look for a completely reversible belt that is a good neutral colour on each side, or even a neutral with a reverse side in a fashion colour that will work with an existing outfit.

Don't stick to always matching your belts to your shoes. For example, if you are wearing a simple dress, set it off with a colour, red for example, that can co-ordinate with the colour of your shoes. Red would work well with navy, taupe or black shoes. If you have mainly warm tones in your shoes, such as brown tones, try an olive or rust belt with your dresses or skirts. Obviously, you will want to tie the colour of the belt in with some-

left: Most skirts look 'unfinished' without a belt, even if they don't have belt loops

right: Polish off your skirts and trousers with an attractive leather belt

thing else, perhaps a fleck of a colour in the skirt or with the colour of your blouse or scarf.

Only wear belts with distinctive buckles and similar features if you have a trim waist worth the attention. Otherwise, it is best to keep the belt simple, in a colour that blends with your skirt or dress.

Self-belts – ones of the same fabric as the dress, skirt or trousers – look less significant than a leather belt. They are rarely of decent quality or construction and often have cheap and shiny gilt buckles. Toss them out as soon as you get them home so you aren't even tempted to wear them.

HOSIERY

Are you a woman who wears one colour with most of your wardrobe? If so, you aren't looking as sophisticated as you could. In most cities and towns, in most countries, hosiery is available in a wide range of textures, colours and fits so that every woman should be able to find a good brand to complete her look for work.

Some supermarket brands or ones purporting to fit any size can look horrible, making some legs look like artificial limbs, and they can be very uncomfortable. My clients moan that buying expensive hosiery is like pouring money down the drain because their tights often expire after one wearing (even upon opening the package!). But if you keep your nails and hands smooth, and are careful in laundering your hosiery there is no reason why tights should not last for many months. The key is to buy quality, to get the right fit and to select the right blend of fibres that are hardwearing (for example, with Lycra).

Getting tights to last is one challenge; the other is getting them to look good. Here's where you need to know your deniers, that is, the appropriate weight for comfort and to compliment your look. Here's a guide to what to look for:

◆ 5, 7, 10, 12 denier: Lightweight for summertime. Hot climates, hot offices

◆ 15–30 denier: Medium weight, for air-cooled offices

◆ 30–60 denier: For wintertime. There is nothing heavier in opaque than 60 denier.

In selecting colours don't aim to contrast with your outfit (for example, wearing white or coloured tights) but to tone in with your skirt, dress or trousers, and with your shoes. So, if you are wearing a navy skirt and navy shoes, beige legs would stand out and break up your look; the best choice would be a sheer navy or a blue-grey. If your skirts and shoes are warm-toned then natural coloured tights or beige are nice. Never try to create the impression of having a tan by wearing 'suntan' hosiery. It never works and cheapens any business look. Patterned hosiery, apart from designs so subtle as to be indistinguishable, has no place in business.

A final note on problem legs. For large, unshapely or marked legs (such as noticeable veins or scars) darker tones are best. For very slim legs, lighter colours create more 'weight' and 'shape'.

SHOES

Many working women have a 'disposable shoe' mentality, that is, they buy one or two pairs of shoes, wear them to death for a few months then throw them away and buy replacements. Generally, they are inexpensive shoes which tend to look slightly beaten up by the third wearing, even if well-polished. They just don't hold their shape like a more expensive model, partly due to the fact that they are usually unlined – and often synthetic.

This book emphasises the importance of buying quality because good quality not only projects your success, how much you value yourself and your job, but is also better value for money. My 'disposable shoe' friends probably spend more on shoes over a year than others who buy better quality and they never experience the joy of looking wonderful and feeling comfortable.

You should have about five pairs of good quality shoes to wear with your business clothes. They don't need to be the same in style or boringly safe. Have some variety in, say, two pairs, but with the majority

1

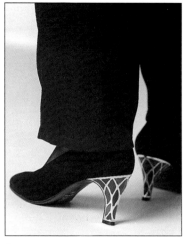

2

1. A medium heel is as high as you should go for business. Tone the colour of your hosiery with your shoes for an elegant finish

2. Colourful details on shoes are distracting and unprofessional. Save them for the disco

3. Metallic shoes, popular in the summertime, aren't acceptable in many industries

4. Stacked heels and shoe-boots are best with trousers rather than skirts

5. Keep the detail on your business shoes to a minimum

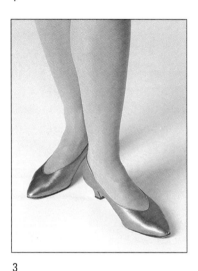

3

4

5

able to work well with any suit. Buy only calf leather or suede for work. In the summer, don't succumb to open-toed, or sandal styles or anything in shiny or patent leather. These styles and materials would weaken your professional image.

Find a good manufacturer/label whose sizes and styles are comfortable on you. We have all at some time experimented with unknown brands and qualities and lived to regret the purchases every time we wear them or because we find we cannot wear them. You can pay a lot of money for poor quality but you can never pay a little and get more (unless you know your way around the wonderful leather outlets of Milan).

No matter if you spend £100 on a pair of shoes today, most of your purchases will require a cobbler's attention before wearing. Heels and upper soles are so thin that if you wear them you risk damaging the upper part of the shoes. Replace the heels with quality leather or rubber as well as the toes or entire soles to ensure their longevity. Also treat any suede or fabric shoes (not a recommended investment) with a weather- or water-resistant spray before wearing. Nothing is as heartbreaking as getting caught in the rain on the first day of wearing new shoes, and have them acquire a permanent water-mark that cannot be concealed even by the most assiduous cleaning or polishing.

Store all your shoes in a cupboard or wardrobe between wearings, using shoe trees to help them keep their shape. Resting shoes for two to three days before wearing them again will allow the leather to recuperate and will help your shoes to last much longer.

Boots should be worn only for practical reasons – either mid-winter to protect your feet from cold or snow – or during torrential rain. (In New York you need 'rubbers' – rubber boots – when it is stormy.) But during inclement weather always keep a pair of normal shoes in the office to look your best. When boots are very much in fashion, try to resist them unless you work in a particularly relaxed environment.

If you habitually walk a good distance to and from the office, by all means be sensible and change your smart business shoes for something more sturdy and comfortable. But don't forget to substitute more appropriate shoes once in the office.

ATTACHÉS, BRIEF-CASES AND HANDBAGS

Working women tend to carry around more clutter than men. We have our business papers in an attaché or folder and all of our personal items – make-up, hair brush, keys and so on in a handbag. So what's the problem? It's simply that coping with two bags makes your comings and goings both clumsy and distracting and for no good reason.

The ideal arrangement is to have one receptacle for everything. If you are one of those women who use their bag as a filing cabinet cum holdall, take yourself firmly in hand. You really can survive without it. And you will. All of your personal bits – a hair brush or comb, powder and lipstick – should be kept in a small make-up case and stored inside your attaché or brief-case along with your diary, wallet, cheque-book, keys, and pen-set. For women who travel by public transport or who are in and out of taxis and needing to get to their wallets easily, a *small* shoulder bag simply to hold your wallet is both acceptable and practical.

When choosing an attaché or brief-case, buy the best you can afford and, preferably, in leather. Manufacturers are very much aware now of the considerable – and still increasing – army of career women, and they are bringing out new designs specifically for us. So shop around until you find one that suits your special needs.

Unless you really do have to carry around large amounts of documentation, weigh in the balance one of the slim-line models – but with a base-line insert that allows reasonable expansion when needed. Bear in mind that leather bags can be heavy even when empty; make sure you will be able to carry yours with ease when it is full. Check the design of the handle, too. Is it comfortable to grip, not too thick yet sturdy enough not to let you down after a year or so of intensive use? Is it retractable so that you can carry it under your arm if and when necessary? While this is not essential, you might find it a useful facility.

Colour choice is still very limited; a few more neutrals could be added to the present ranges. However, black or a warm reddish-brown look smart with most businesswear; if navy is your main basic colour, you should be able to find this, too.

If you hate hard attachés and brief-cases, and prefer a shoulder bag, look at attractive ones referred to as 'Shopping Bags' but which, in leather and with a price tag usually starting out around £100, are anything but! This style is very versatile in that you can carry papers for most meetings (it should be big enough to hold a normal file folder and pad of paper) and usually has handy zip compartments for personal items. If it has an adjustable strap, so much the better. Constantly carrying a heavy shoulder bag can be very wearing, not only for you but for your jacket. On occasions you might prefer to carry it as a 'grip'.

Men in business judge each other's status by their attachés or brief-cases. Increasingly, women do, too. Make sure your preferred style is both functional and as impressive as you can afford.

SCARVES AND SHAWLS

If you have yet to discover the wonders of scarves as a means to be more colourful and interesting, come to London and visit Liberty's – scarf heaven! After you recover from the excitement of all the colours you'll be taken by the patterns – some ethnic, others soft and floral or vibrant blends of texture, colour and abstraction. You won't be able to resist one.

Again, you should begin by choosing scarves and shawls that compliment **you** first in terms of colouring, scale and personality. Once you've got your focus on a few, think of wearing the scarf with a simple dress or jacket. Obviously, it will be advisable to wear the dress or suit when you try on the scarf, if you plan to invest in an expensive one.

If you find scarves fiddly and can't stand the fuss with them moving

1. Fold a medium-sized scarf (35½ inches / 90cm square is ideal) in half to make a triangle. Centre the triangle, hanging point down, under the neck. Cross the ends behind the neck and bring down in front, over the triangle

2. Adjust to suit your neck and collar, then tie . . .

3. . . . in a double knot or secure with a small brooch

Scarves can transform the most basic outfits. Choose colours from your palette to complement your wardrobe. Select patterns in balance with your scale and that suit your personality

about, you might consider larger shawls to wear with your jackets. Whichever shawl you choose can be secured with a pin to prevent it sliding from your shoulders. Silk scarves are more troublesome for the uninitiated scarf-wearer because they slide about more than wool ones.

See the illustrations here for basic but undeniably stylish ways to wear scarves with confidence. There's no better way to compliment a new suit or coat, or to make older ones look new and exciting.

Your make-up polish

Studies in America as well as in Europe bear out the fact that women who wear make-up to work not only stand a good chance of getting ahead of female colleagues who don't, but tend to earn more money and be promoted faster. Similar research was carried out in the mid-1980s

1

2

3

1. Women in business who don't wear make-up look unpolished and unprofessional

2. Taking short cuts always shows. A dab of lipstick, blush and mascara evaporates by mid morning, leaving you looking bare, tired or ill

3. It takes 10 minutes in the morning to complete a professional make-up that will last all day (aside from touching up your powder and lipstick). The results convey the right message: polished, professional and in charge

by Clairol in America and Drs. Jouhar and Graham in Britain to see whether a woman's make-up and hair style – or grooming – had any influence on employers. Photographs and CVs were sent out to top personnel officers, some showing the candidates wearing make-up and others without. The results showed that not only were the candidates wearing make-up more likely to be offered jobs but they were offered salaries up to 20 per cent higher.

When I cite these studies some of my female clients wince, resenting that they are judged unfairly not only on merit and their abilities but also on other more personally demanding standards than men in business. However, the fact that you are reading this book suggests that you have accepted that image *is* a key factor in your career progression. Make-up just happens to be an additional factor for women. While men with beards may be unduly prejudiced against when job-seeking, so, too, are women who neglect to wear make-up.

The good news, if you hate wearing make-up, is that you should look as if you are wearing very little. Our studies have shown that women who wear too much make-up, garish colours and heavy techniques, are considered to have a poorer image than a woman without. But the woman who looks fresh, natural and polished in a subtle make-up that compliments her wins hands-down every time.

DOES YOUR MAKE-UP DATE YOU?

Chances are, if you have ever been interested in eye-shadows and lipsticks, you learned how to apply make-up in your late teens and early twenties. Techniques learned then are generally still applied by women in their thirties, forties, fifties and beyond.

It is all too easy for others to tell when you were in your prime simply by how you wear your make-up now. Heavy-handed black eyeliner screams that you left school in the early 1970s. Blue eye-shadow dates you to the late 50s. Pale, frosted pink lips and thick mascara are 1960s vintage. Going without foundation but treating your entire face to the shiny look is a hallmark of leaving school in the early 1980s. *Are* you unwittingly adding years to your age simply because you haven't learned how to apply make-up using up-to-date colours and techniques?

True, a trip to the cosmetics section or counter at a good department store can be daunting; the beauty assistants tend to look too perfect, almost unreal. They probably spent no less than an hour making themselves up, have 10 to 15 different products on their faces and need great perseverance to get it off in the evenings. This is not what I mean by Power Polish.

No, to learn what is right for you, visit a make-up artist or image consultant who doesn't mind you bringing along your own make-up and will teach you how to do your own face, and suggest any other products that would further enhance your individual looks. Anyone can paint you up to look wonderful. The art is to *teach* you how to do it yourself. A perfect polish for business requires a simple method and some basic techniques that take no longer than 10 minutes each morning.

COLOURS THAT WORK FOR YOU

According to your colouring, select make-up shades that help you look healthy and well-groomed. Aim to compliment your own natural skintone, eye and hair colour. Worry less about co-ordinating your eye-shadows with your outfits and concentrate rather on looking natural. A few, well-chosen colours will work with most of your wardrobe, and your make-up will help you achieve more in business if you use it to enhance your features as tools vital to communication.

You want a clear, healthy complexion, not one artificially coloured to look darker, lighter, pinker or peachier than you are. Regardless of your age or the quality of your natural complexion, you can radiate health and vitality simply by choosing the right foundation, also judiciously using a small amount of concealer if necessary, then setting it with a colourless translucent powder and lightly applying a dash of a natural blush colour.

Draw attention to your eyes – not with bright colours in your eye-shadows, liners or mascara but by subtle definition, 'framing' them with rich, almost neutral shades and emphasising the colours in your irises.

Your mouth should project confidence and vigour, and should be touched-up with a lipstick periodically throughout the day. Most women have strong feelings about the lipstick colours they prefer. For instance, while a red lipstick is needed when you wear red in your outfit, it is the preserve of only the most confident women. So many business women I have worked with recoil at the suggestion of wearing a red lipstick. If unaccustomed to wearing lipstick regularly, start with a more natural tone that compliments the colours of your palette.

If your colouring is essentially 'warm' a salmon, terracotta, or warm pink will work with most things. If you have 'cool' colouring try a wine, deep rose or soft mauve. Very light, pale or pearlised/frosted lipsticks are not business-like. Go for colours that are medium in depth, not too dark, and matt in finish.

MAKE-UP TIPS FOR WORKING WOMEN

◆ Select a foundation that matches the colour of your skintone along the jawline.

◆ Use a lighter foundation than your normal colour or concealer on dark patches (around the eyes, corners of the nose, on the chin) to look fresher and achieve a more even complexion.

◆ If blusher disappears on you, try using a cream blusher *before* you powder, then add a soft dash of powder blusher on top.

◆ Apply loose translucent powder to set your foundation using a powder puff or by pressing in with cotton wool. Within minutes it will be absorbed.

◆ A light eye-base applied all over the lid before any eye-shadow helps your eye-shadow last 12 hours or more without creasing.

◆ Use soft, neutral colours for your eye-shadow. Apply peach or a soft pink as a base and use a rich brown or grey to define and give the eyes depth.

◆ Use a soft taupe or brown eye-shadow, lighter than the colour of your own eyebrows, to fill in any uneven patches (more natural looking than using pencil).

◆ Use a little clear mascara or hair gel on a comb to brush eyebrows up and into place.

◆ A soft line along the outer third of your top and lower eyelids, using a rich kohl pencil, makes your eyelashes look thicker.

◆ Apply lip pencil in a natural colour all over your lips before using your lipstick – it helps your lipstick last much longer.

◆ Touch up your powder and lipstick a couple of times during the working day.

◆ Try not to touch your face excessively.

GO ON, SMILE!

Second only to your eyes, your mouth is a central focus in communication. How naturally do you use and express yourself with your mouth when you speak, and when you smile?

Many people develop strained, controlled mouth movements to hide embarrassing teeth. But the effect of such antics only convey other negative signals about your personality and confidence which may be far more detrimental to your image than your chipped, stained or missing teeth. If your teeth and gums aren't healthy or attractive there are several affordable remedies you should consider.

BRIGHTEN YOUR SMILE WITH WHITER TEETH

Most adults experience tooth discoloration as part of the ageing process, but tea, coffee, alcohol and smoking all make it worse. Special toothpastes can remove stains and prevent new ones with regular use. For those who want really gleaming teeth **cosmetic bleaching** is an option. A special cosmetic dentist takes an impression of your mouth and makes a mouth guard which contains a small amount of non-toxic bleach. The

Before cosmetic dental treatment   After treatment

guard needs to be worn for one hour a day and takes between 3 and 6 weeks to reach the desired state of whiteness.

FILLING UNSIGHTLY GAPS AND CRACKS

Gaps or chipped teeth can make you look older and unhealthy but they can easily be rectified by a qualified cosmetic dentist in a matter of weeks.

Veneers of a thin porcelain facing can be used to cover unsightly stained or chipped teeth, or improve the alignment of crooked teeth. These veneers are very strong and natural looking.

For smaller gaps or chips, **bonding and contouring** may be used. A putty-like material is added to the tooth then moulded and set with ultra-violet light.

Cosmetic **crowns and bridges** should be considered for replacing missing teeth or to cover teeth crumbling from overfilling or broken beyond benefiting from bonding. A crown is an individual porcelain tooth that is fitted over an existing damaged or unsightly tooth. The existing tooth is reduced to accommodate it. A bridge is used to replace missing teeth and requires the teeth on either side of the gap to be reduced and cemented with a fixture to keep the dummy tooth or teeth in place. While more complicated, getting a bridge is far preferable to dentures.

Another method of replacing missing teeth is with implants. The advantage of implants is that adjacent teeth to the gap aren't affected in any way.

If you feel the least self-conscious about your teeth, consult your dentist on the possibilities of cosmetic dentistry. If she says that you are imagining the problem, don't stop there. Your dentist might not be a qualified cosmetic dentist and be too embarrassed to say so or professional enough to recommend someone who can help. You want to find a trained and recognised cosmetic dentist who will gladly give you references, show photographs of clients before and after treatments, and who ideally has spent time training in America which has the state-of-the-art techniques and treatments.

YOUR HAIR

You know how wonderful you feel on a day when your hair looks good and how miserable you feel, no matter how well-dressed, if it isn't up to par. But as a busy working woman you need a hairstyle that you can maintain yourself. Gone are the days when we women visited the hairdresser for a regular 'shampoo and set'. We don't have the time to while away at a salon, nor is more than the four to six weekly trim and treatment affordable for most of us.

So, how well does the colour, cut and style of *your* hair compliment your business image? Be honest. Consider how it looks most days. If you spend good money on your clothes but don't bother to frame your face with an attractive hairstyle, you aren't doing yourself justice. Look back to Ruth on page 99. Before her hair was restyled she looked underconfident and timid because her hair was hiding her face. The right style makes the most of your features and adds power to your presence. Here are the factors you need to consider.

YOUR FACE SHAPE

You will want a style that compliments the shape and features of your face. Pull your hair back and look in the mirror. How would you describe the shape of your face? Does any part of your face predominate – your jaw line, cheekbones, or forehead?

If you don't have a symmetrical oval face (which looks good in just about any style) you need to soften areas of your face that are the strongest and draw attention elsewhere to create balance.

◆ The last thing a woman with a wide jaw wants is a sharp bob that ends at her jawline. She wants to add height to the top, say with a soft, angled fringe or layers on the crown, and to soften her jawline with length in the back but little around the face.

◆ A very round face doesn't want a lot of curls around the cheeks but rather a sleek, pulled-back or long style to minimise the fullness.

◆ A long, oblong face looks even longer if you have long, straight hair. Styles that are full at the sides are more flattering.

If your hairdresser can't advise you on how to compliment your face shape with an appropriate cut and styling, then it is time to find a stylist who can.

THE COLOUR

Many women benefit from enhancing the natural colour of their hair with a semi-permanent rinse or permanent dye. High-lights and low-lights can look wonderfully natural and are especially recommended for women who consider their own hair colour 'mousey'.

Guidelines we give to women when looking for a new hair colour is to go with nature. If you weren't ever a blonde, the chances are you will not look good with blonde high-lights. If your hair gets 'ash' high-lights when you are out in the sunshine, then dyeing your hair red will look ghastly. Any new colour should make you look natural and healthy. One that makes you look pale, fights with your eyebrows or takes all the sparkle out of your eyes isn't worth it, no matter what the fashion magazines declare to be the 'latest' hair colour.

Don't rely on your favourite hairdresser for the best advice on a new hair colour. See a 'colourist' to discuss your concerns and to get it right. A professional colourist will charge you more but at least you shouldn't end up looking ancient or as if you are wearing a wig – too often the result of a trial and error session at the local salon. If you have a large department store within easy travelling distance, you could carry out your own colour and style trial, by trying on a few wigs in the colour and style/s you have in mind.

TEXTURE

Some women are blessed with hair that can dry naturally and look wonderful. Most of us, however, rely on the 'miracle' treatments available today to help improve the texture of our natural manes – perms to add body or curls; mousses and gels to add shape to the limpest hair; as well as oils, waxes and conditioners to improve its natural state. Certainly, given the range of treatments available, you have no excuse today for not making the most of your hair. So take a look in the mirror and ask yourself if you could look slimmer, and younger, with a new style. Give it a go. A terrific new style can do as much to change your image as a new suit – and is much less expensive.

CHAPTER 9

Fit for Success

In the last few years there has been a redefinition of what it takes to project success. Not only do you need to look smart but you must also look healthy. Being fit and 'in shape' has become a metaphor for being in control of yourself. The logic extends to being in control of your career and therefore successful.

Sedentary readers may be ready to flip to another section. 'Spare me another lecture about losing weight, taking up jogging or pumping iron. I am too busy and, quite frankly, beyond it.' But take heart; the experts no longer recommend vigorous, sweaty pursuits as the only way to tone-up but small changes to your sedentary lifestyle that can strengthen your vital organs (your heart especially), make you look more alert – and feel more energetic.

FAT IS A DISCRIMINATORY ISSUE

How do you define someone who looks unhealthy? The scales don't tell the complete story. Many large women who, according to slimming experts, are 'overweight', are actually very fit and healthy but technically do not conform to standards of desirable weights for certain heights and bone structures. A person who is skinny and puny can also be unfit and have an unhealthy lifestyle. It is just that 'overweight' women are considered to be responsible for their condition. The usual argument goes that they ate themselves into their state and they are therefore judged harshly if they don't get themselves back into a condition valued as 'ideal'.

It is a fact that overweight people are discriminated against at work. In a survey we conducted of Britain's top 200 companies, in 1992, personnel and financial directors ranked looking 'fit and healthy' as the second key factor in hiring people (just behind a smart appearance). They defined 'fit' as trim and not overweight. A widely-held perception in business and public life is that the overweight just let themselves go, and if they lack self-control how can they be expected to deliver on the job? They won't be as exacting nor as persevering as their fitter colleagues. If they can't even plan what they eat to get their weight under control, how can they be relied upon to plan anything else?

The prejudice goes on, and sooner or later the overweight find their careers get blocked. For example, if deciding which of two equally competent people should be sent overnight to New York on the 'Red-Eye' for the morning presentation, you can bet that the 'fitter', slimmer person gets the opportunity.

Unlike sex and race discrimination, there is no legislation about discrimination against overweight people, except in the State of California – where it is illegal to discriminate in hiring just on the basis of how a person looks – and that covers the unattractive as well as the overweight. If you don't look healthy and are substantially overweight you will probably be subjected to discrimination in your career, if you haven't been already. You will miss out on potential job advancement, new opportunities and, possibly, the pay you deserve because you don't have what the business world today considers a Successful Image. The right clothes can help but they can't hide a body that most consider only in pejorative terms.

THE SECRET OF WEIGHT CONTROL

Most women who are slaves to diets are basically miserable and can't accept themselves for who they are. You might be overweight and want to lose excess pounds, but dieting isn't the way to long term weight control.

We each have a predetermined natural body weight, and if we try to fall below it we feel ill, weak and invariably give up trying to maintain our desired weight. Most diets cause you to crave sugar, to become mildly or acutely hypoglycaemic. This will cause you to eat, and once you start it becomes difficult to stop. The bottom-line is that 95 per cent of dieters regain the previously lost weight after all the struggle and upset of their weight-loss regime. Many actually put on more than they lost because their basic metabolism has adjusted to the lower food intake.

So, forget about weighing yourself and stop dieting. Avoid quick-fix approaches to getting slim. Most diets focus on food – what types to eat and how much, involving you in weighing and combining schemes that almost become full-time jobs to maintain. Instead, reconsider your *attitude* towards food. If you eat when you aren't hungry, if you gorge on things you know are harmfully 'fattening', then you are in self-destructive mode with an unnatural focus on and unhealthy attitude towards food. If you consider yourself to be a sensible person, you only need to develop a sensible approach to living which includes what, how and when you eat.

Here are ten simple guidelines which most of today's diet and fitness gurus concur can radically transform your weight as well as make you feel wonderful. The best thing about them is that they are easy to remember and simple to follow so they're perfect for today's busy working women.

◆ Don't skip meals.

◆ Eat smaller amounts, four to five times a day rather than three large meals.

◆ Drink a litre of mineral or filtered water daily to help eliminate the build-up of harmful toxins which trap fluids and fat.

◆ Avoid fried foods and those with a high fat content. Use olive oil (you need less and digest it more easily than animal or vegetable oil) in cooking or dressings.

◆ Try eating one meal of just vegetables or fruit daily, to treat your body to essential natural nutrients for energy and health, and to 'flush out' your system.

◆ Avoid soft, fizzy or caffeine drinks.

◆ Don't eat after 8pm unless it's a special occasion. Try to keep the evening meal the lightest of the day.

◆ Sit down to eat, and chew slowly and thoroughly. Don't watch TV or read a book at the same time. Concentrate on your food and savour every mouthful.

◆ Don't add sugar or salt to your food; apart from a little salt when cooking.

◆ Have three alcohol-free days a week.

You know how to eat healthily. No one needs to tell you to cut out sweets, biscuits, chocolate and highly processed foods in order to stay trim. You don't need to count calories. Neither starve yourself nor gorge yourself. Enjoy your meals, keeping an honest appraisal of what you are eating. Simply return to healthy eating and befriend yourself as you are. You'll be surprised how soon those skirts begin to feel comfortable, how much better you will feel, and how terrific you will look.

STAYING FIT WITH EXERCISE

If it has been a while since you had a complete physical and you don't know exactly how fit you are for your age, why not book an appointment with your doctor or at a fitness assessment clinic – a medical one, not your local gym. Most private health insurers have these clinics, and are usually willing to provide this check-up service even if you are not a member of their scheme. The service does not come cheap; but it is worth the price.

The American fitness guru, Dr Kenneth Cooper (the man who coined 'aerobics'), recommends a fitness stress test as part of any annual physical. This is where you are linked up to an electro-cardiogram while doing exercises such as walking, riding an exercise bicycle or running on a treadmill. By means of this test, doctors can see if any of the arteries to the heart are under strain or blocked. Even if you are a 'fitness freak', after 40 you should have this test done every two years, according to Cooper.

After a good physical check-up, it's time to analyse your activity level and develop a fitness programme to suit your lifestyle. You don't need to take out an expensive membership to a Health Club or buy a new wardrobe of Lycra leotards to get your fitness under control. You can build it into your life by changing your behaviour throughout the regular working day. It is the extent to which you move your body and are active throughout the day that determines your fitness, as much as any regular workout programme. Walking, climbing stairs and lifting things – rather than resorting to all the modern conveniences available to avoid activity, like cars and lifts – can keep you as fit as you need to be.

If you are a newcomer to regular exercise, you are advised to take it slowly but to do some moderate activity for gradually longer periods. Rather than a ten minute dash around the park in the morning, walk 20 or 30 minutes to the office (get off the train a stop or two early or park your car further away). Do this three or four days a week and you will have a fitter body in six months.

Dr Kenneth Cooper, who directs the Cooper Aerobics Institute in Dallas, has studied the correlation between death and fitness among business-people who came to his clinic for health checks. The greatest number of fatalities were among those who took no exercise. However, the people who took 'some regular exercise' had a significantly improved lifespan.

So with just a little effort you can not only look and feel better but you can live longer. Fitness helps you fight off the degenerative processes of ageing, such as heart disease, high blood pressure, and stiff joints. You can have a say in how fast you age. Fit and healthy women in their forties can have the vitality of sedentary colleagues 10 to 15 years younger, and often enjoy even more energy. So fitness can help the insecure middle-aged women threatened by younger talent vying for their jobs, by keeping a few paces ahead – both literally and figuratively!

WALK BEFORE YOU RUN

Walking, a favoured pastime throughout Europe, is now a sport, and is the best exercise for the uninitiated. In America, walking clubs have popped up everywhere. Jane Fonda and other fitness gurus actually do videos on how to walk. It is important, of course, to wear specially designed 'walking' shoes, not the ones you think of when you head to the hills, but trainers with special soles and construction to facilitate street-walking. You don't need to spend money on designer models, but you do need comfortable shoes with inbuilt support in the right places to make the most of walking and to encourage you to go for longer stints.

Walking is much safer than running and more practicable for working people because it is a part of everyday life. But make sure you know 'how to walk', so you get the most out of the activity. Shuffling about or walking all hunched up doesn't make the most of the exercise. Keep your shoulders back to allow the lungs to function fully. Next, thrust the pelvis slightly forward – just a little more than you normally would – to allow full movement of the hips; you want them to roll easily from side to side as you walk. It is preferable to walk unencumbered letting your arms swing slightly as you move. Consider a back-pack to carry your gear to and from the office (keeping your smart attaché or brief-case in your desk for use at meetings throughout the day).

Use your whole foot when you walk. Feel your toes, land your heel first then roll your sole forward. Use your ankles. Stretch your stride. The longer the stride the greater the effort, and the more muscles you will stretch throughout your body. A good walk engages your whole body as well as your mind and, eventually, your spirit. If you build more walking into your daily life, you'll feel and look fitter in no time.

THAT BEAUTIFUL BUZZ

Exercise is beneficial not simply to help burn calories and to keep your weight down but also to improve performance dramatically in areas as diverse as concentration, IQ, and muscle endurance (not to mention fertility and sexual performance!). Speak with any of your fit colleagues and ask them why they are so active and they will tell you it is for the *feeling* they get during and after activity that they keep it up – not to lose weight necessarily.

Go for that same feeling, that wonderful *buzz*. You will find that anything bothering you before a good walk or a visit to the gym, evaporates within minutes. Exercise makes you think more clearly, it gets your worries into perspective. You can be tied-up in knots over a problem and find yourself laughing it off after a workout. No drink, no drug enables you to do that and still function at the top of your form, but exercise does!

CHAPTER 10

Presenting Yourself

Sooner or later you will have to face the challenge of speaking to an audience. All successful women know that their career progression, to a significant extent, is based upon their exposure. Being seen and heard both inside and outside your organisation helps to increase your profile as well as your prospects.

To turn down opportunities to gain visibility is shooting yourself in the career foot. If you find the prospect of public-speaking daunting, take heart from the fact that most professionals are nervous when speaking to an audience.

If in real doubt about your ability, or simply interested in improving your techniques, consider taking a good training course; it is one of the best investments you can make to advance your career. The objective of so-called Communications Skills training is not simply to learn how to prepare and deliver a talk but also how to enjoy the experience and to be yourself.

Although technically you will be giving a presentation on a specific subject, remember what you are also doing is presenting yourself. Within the first three minutes or so of speaking, your audience will decide whether or not they'll bother to listen. That is why so many books and training programmes on presentation skills stress the importance of a good opening. But just as important as what you say and how you say it, is your image.

Depending on the size of the presentation or whether or not you are appearing on video or TV, you will need different advice. So let's set the stage for some key presentation situations you might encounter and give you guidelines that can be adapted to any similar situations in which you might find yourself.

THE INTERNAL MEETING, UP TO 15 PEOPLE

A small business presentation might be made at a formal board meeting or in a less formal situation, such as a training session. The two key questions to ask are:

◆ *What is the purpose of the presentation?*
  Are you there to inform and not invite much participation?
  Or are you there to present ideas for discussion?

◆ *Who is the audience?*
  Internal colleagues? Peers, subordinates, or supervisors? Clients or potential customers? The press? The general public?

THE FORMAL PRESENTATION

When your purpose is primarily to inform your audience and not to elicit discussion you want to project authority – conservatism in your appearance and confidence in your behaviour. Here are some tips to consider:

What to wear

Think classic. There should be nothing fussy about your appearance. Select the darkest suit you can wear and still look healthy and interesting. Wear a simple blouse underneath. Finish the look with a striking necklace and strong earrings.

Check the fit of the suit when buttoned, because that is how you must wear it when you give a formal presentation. If you are full-busted or full-figured, be sure the fit is easy and loose.

Your hair should be well-groomed and not require you to fidget with it constantly. If uncertain about its manageability, use a hairspray on the morning of an important presentation.

Your body language

Your gestures, behaviour and voice need to be as convincing as the words you use. Avoid defensive postures such as holding your hands behind your back, 'hugging' yourself or crossing your arms in front of yourself which only convey your defensiveness and concern about what you are saying.

Keep your body *open*. If using notes, keep one hand at your side, or use natural hand movements with your palms up. Also, don't let your gestures *preach*, that is, use a pointing finger to make a point or, if seated at a table, fold your hands and make a steeple with your fingers (which conveys arrogance!).

Regardless of how serious the subject may be, the occasional smile (not grin) will help you to win acceptance. Use eye contact with everyone in the room, regularly and deliberately, as if you are speaking to each person directly. And don't avoid eye contact with any detractors. Meeting them head on will show you are confident and may even stifle other possible challenges.

Sending the wrong signals: Formal presentations demand authority dressing. A light-pink suit and floral blouse lack authority. Always button your jacket before presenting to keep the attention on your face. If you wear glasses and present frequently, get non-reflective lenses

You will hold attention better and look more credible in a high-confidence colour combination from your personal palette (see Chapter 4) like navy and ivory, and an elegant style. Significant, never fussy, accessories complete the professional polish

Make sure your voice is convincing; end all your declarations in a low tone, as if what you have said is a statement of fact.

THE INFORMAL PRESENTATION

In a more relaxed environment or when you want people to open up and participate you require to show less authority in dress and behaviour, but more personality and selfless consideration of others' opinions. A training seminar, staff meeting or brainstorming session would be examples. For these, appear open, welcoming. Here's what to consider:

What to wear

Select less severe colours and styles. So rather than the navy suit (the matching jacket and skirt, so appropriate for a formal presentation), try a lighter neutral, perhaps a taupe jacket over a red or turquoise dress; or team the jacket with a patterned skirt. Here's where you can have more freedom with colours you enjoy wearing. But remember that you are still conducting the meeting and you need to be pleasing to watch. Don't bombard your audience with excessive patterns or distracting features such as a scarf that slides around, or wisps of hair straying in your face which need constant fixing.

Your body language

You also need to behave differently than when in more formal situations. Your questions will be open to elicit discussion; so, too, should be your gestures. Don't stand rigid, glued to one spot at the head of the table. Move around, extend your hand to invite people to speak. Touch people on the shoulder or arm, if appropriate, to reinforce what they have said or to bring them into the discussion. Sit down from time to time when others are speaking to 'give them the floor', to signal that what they are contributing merits everyone's attention, including yours.

Be an active listener when others are speaking. Keep your eyes on them as if what they are saying is vital and compelling. Take notes and reiterate key points that the participants make. Nod your head when you agree. When you don't, try to take it on board without showing your feelings. Allow others to rebuff contrary viewpoints from time to time, rather than always being the one to defend or take issue with difficult points.

The ability to run an informal meeting is essential to building your reputation and maintaining a rapport among your colleagues, subordinates and managers. Develop a style that makes everyone feel good about participating while still maintaining distinction as the woman at the helm.

LARGE AUDIENCE PRESENTATIONS

Speaking to a group of over 15 people becomes a performance. In addition to being a capable and talented professional you must now move into the area of entertainment. No, I am *not* recommending tedious jokes as the way to enliven a presentation. But you do need to capture your audience and hold its attention not only with your speech but also with your image. When a great package holds a terrific product you've got a winning combination. And whether you are a sales representative or selling yourself and your talents, the rules are the same.

YOU ARE THE KEY PROP

A good presentation to a large audience is never just verbal; it always requires good visual aids. Any audience today expects images to help convey the messages. On average, they will have seen two hours of television a day, have been bombarded with slick commercial advertising while driving to work, read newspapers and business material, and have probably taken a presentation course impressing upon them the importance of visual aids! Props are needed to enliven a large presentation as well as to help organise and enhance your message. But always remember that your Number One Prop is **yourself**.

For a large audience presentation you need to think theatre: project your voice, preferably via a microphone and enlarge your gestures to correlate with the size of your audience. But additionally you need to draw attention to yourself and help hold the audience's gaze through your appearance.

You also need to do a lot of homework. I am not referring to your speech here, but the logistics of the presentation: without knowing in advance the room layout, staging, background, lighting, etc., your appearance may fail completely.

ROOM LAYOUT

It's essential to learn the layout of the room to discern how visible you'll be to the majority of the audience. If speaking from the floor – at the same level as your audience – be sure you are tall enough to be seen. Women need to watch this in particular. I'm only 5ft 3inches and regularly insist on having a platform to speak from so people can see all of me. Otherwise, you simply become a talking head, which hardly provides enough visual animation to keep your audience's gaze.

Once I didn't have the opportunity to see a location for an important presentation. The dining room was packed and the head table, where I was seated, was in front and under poor light. Flanked by people who towered over me, whose own presentations went off fine, I knew I was doomed when it came time to speak. Then, just as I was being introduced I noticed a central stair well leading to the dining room. With outward calm I made my way up to the top of the stairs, asked everyone to adjust their seats and spoke from there. Despite having the after dinner 'graveyard slot', I not only succeeded in really grabbing their attention, but managed to hold it for most of the time! But try to avoid such last minute manoeuvres by seeing the venue beforehand, whenever possible.

STAGING

At formal conferences, you can expect to be on stage either seated at a table or introduced and left at a lectern, from which you deliver your speech. In either event, be sure that your clothes don't let you down.

Watch that your skirt doesn't ride-up and that it's comfortable enough to sit with your knees together and feet both to one side. If you must cross your legs do so only at the ankles.

At the podium or lectern make sure your entire face, at least, is seen. Ideally, you should be visible down to your bust, to hold your audience's attention.

Formal, prepared speeches usually put audiences to sleep unless they are under 10 minutes in duration. If you don't have the time to commit your talk to memory, can't 'wing-it' with cue-cards or an outline, and find an autocue nerve-wracking, then break the presentation up at points which allow you to move slightly away from the lectern (assuming the microphone can still pick you up) and speak seemingly extemporaneously. Aim to be seen in full, once or twice, to break up the monotony of being a talking head.

Try making your introduction away from the lectern, in a more natural way, to impress the audience with your confidence and attract them with your appearance. Then retreat to the lectern to give your speech. At the end, come back and present yourself to the audience with a closing remark.

BACKGROUND

Essential to ensuring that you stand out and are clearly seen during a large platform presentation is to find out the colour of the backdrop. Often, this consists of very dark curtains and if you are standing in front in a dark outfit you simply disappear. Aim to dress in complementary contrast to your backdrop.

LIGHTING

It might seem an obvious point that you need a spotlight on you to be seen, but how often have you noticed someone speaking in almost total darkness, particularly when delivering a slide presentation. Those little lectern lights which simply help you read your notes aren't enough. You need to be well-lit the entire time, if you are to hold your audience's attention.

Lighting comes in a variety of blue and yellow tones. If speaking somewhere other than at a modern business conference facility, check out what kind of lights they use. If the lights are very blue and you are in a navy suit and blue shirt you'll fade away. If the lighting is extreme, either very blue or very yellow, be sure you balance your suit and shirt to contrast with them. Stage technicians are often very helpful.

Don't allow your visual aids to dominate your platform. Be sure to have a spotlight on you when using slides

WHAT TO WEAR

Remember that, unlike at the small presentation, the large audience is theatre. Hence, you need to think of the impact of your 'costume'.

For a large presentation, your best red will project confidence (even if your knees are banging) and hold the audience's attention. Your make-up needs to be stronger and more defined than usual and if wearing red, always wear a matching or toning red lipstick. Earrings are the essential accessory. Be sure your hair is controlled, off your face and perfectly smooth. If it is below shoulder-length, put it up in an elegant French plait or twist.

TIPS ON PRESENTING YOURSELF

◆ Empty all your pockets so your suit lies flat and there are no unseemly bulges.

◆ Button up your jacket, otherwise the eyes will focus on your midriff, perhaps not your most flattering point.

◆ Avoid fussy details, like dangling or bright jewellery.

◆ Draw the attention to your face. Keep dark colours or neutrals below waist level and don't draw attention to your legs or shoes with light colours.

◆ Avoid wearing glasses, if possible. If they *are* needed, then be sure that your eyes are seen at the centre of the lens (no half glasses). And the glasses will be best if given a non-reflective treatment to prevent the 'light spot' glare.

◆ Check beforehand that your hair is well groomed. Spray any unruly and stray hairs into place.

◆ Wear stronger make-up than normal, paying specific attention to defining your eyes (with liner, mascara and combed brows), and emphasise your lips. Use a lip-liner before applying your lipstick to give definition and help the lipstick to last. Powder your face liberally with translucent powder to minimise shining, and press it lightly but firmly into your foundation. Avoid a too-powdered look.

THE IMAGE OF YOUR VOICE

The success of many politicians, actors and business-people can to some extent be attributed to the quality of their voices. Think for a minute of the voices you admire. The radio gives us many opportunities to hear some splendid examples with whom we are all familiar.

When I mention the names of some famous people you can immediately **hear** them: Eddie Murphy, Her Majesty the Queen, the late Marilyn Monroe and Richard Burton, TV presenter Oprah Winfrey. Their voices are distinctive – and integral to their personalities. If Richard Burton had had John Major's voice would he have been such a successful actor? Would Mr Major's political fortunes be different if he could speak to us like Richard Burton? Would Marilyn Monroe have been as sexy with Hillary Clinton's voice?

What impression does your voice leave with other people? This is an important consideration because your voice accounts for 38 per cent of the impression you make on people; 55 per cent depends on how you look and behave and only 7 per cent on what you are saying. I'm not suggesting, however, that if you look, act and sound wonderful you can speak rubbish. Of course not. Your words are vital. But in business and politics we have to assume you know what you are talking about (or someone can back you up). So, it becomes more a question of how you sell your message. If you can't sell your ideas you can't succeed in business or public life.

A good voice enhances your power of persuasion, in addition to keeping your audience's attention when you speak. A bad voice at best bores and at worst irritates, undermining the otherwise favourable image that you have worked so hard to develop.

IS YOUR VOICE IN-TUNE?

Think of your own voice. If any of the following problems sound familiar when you get up and speak, then some work is required to improve your voice.

◆ You feel unnatural when speaking and hear a different voice, usually higher than your normal conversational tone.

◆ You're an adult but your voice sounds adolescent. Sometimes people ring you at home and ask to speak to your mummy.

◆ People ask you to 'speak up', even when you are speaking in only a small gathering.

◆ You use 'fillers' when you speak: 'um', 'right', 'you know', 'and so forth'.

◆ You sound flat when speaking through a microphone.

◆ Your voice gets tired and throat hurts after speaking for 15 or 20 minutes.

◆ You have a strong regional accent not widely understood. People often say, 'excuse me, could you repeat that?'

◆ You finish sentences high, as if you are asking a question when you are actually stating a fact.

◆ You don't sound authoritative.

◆ You simply don't like the sound of your voice!

IMPROVING YOUR VOICE

First, be assured that you are not condemned for life to having an indifferent or poor voice. You can do something about it.

Your voice is mainly conditioned by your experience: how and where you grew up, where your parents were from, the schools you attended, the children you hung around with. As an adult, other influences will have come into play: how much you have travelled, your colleagues at work and how they speak, the programmes you watch on television or listen to on the radio, and your partner's voice.

Before reaching for the trade phone directory to find a speech therapist, there are several things you can do on your own to improve your voice that don't cost anything. Here's where to start.

◆ Ask your friends and closest colleagues what they like about your voice and what they find irritating. Tell them how you would like to sound. For example, you might wish that your voice could be described as: clear, rich, authoritative, lively, pleasing, reassuring, confident, friendly, intelligent, natural.

◆ Practise reading out loud, trying to be more expressive and improve your pronunciation, pace and modulation.

◆ If possible, read to children. They are the most honest audience you will ever get. If you keep their attention you are doing well. If they start to fidget and stop listening, you've lost. Ask them if they like your voice and, whether you hear an enthusiastic 'Yes', or a definite 'No', ask them why.

◆ Record your voice on to a tape recorder. Do short 3 minute 'speeches', pretending you are being interviewed on the radio on something about which you can speak off the cuff, such as the trip to work this morning; what you enjoyed about a recent film; describing your favourite restaurant. Listen carefully to the playback and aim to improve the next recording by what you learned on previous ones.

Don't erase the tape. Keep it as a record to monitor your progress. The sort of faults you can easily detect yourself are those of unattractive pitch, ums and ahs, lack of variety in pace of delivery, lack of clarity.

PREPARING YOUR VOICE FOR A PRESENTATION

So, you have worked to improve your voice and it's now time actually to get up and speak. Most presenters get nervous, so you are not alone.

Here's what you need to do to control your nerves and allow your voice to project as well as possible.

Relax

The adrenalin is pumping through your body as you wait for your turn to speak. This is when you can tense-up from head to toe. If your body tenses you can bet that your throat seizes up as well.

To avoid this, try to exercise the night before, or better still the morning of a big presentation. This should include a good workout, say, either running, swimming or cycling, and some stretching exercises. Before you speak, go for a brisk walk wherever you can; around the block, up and down a few flights of stairs, through the lobby of the conference centre. Brisk movement before you begin speaking allows the adrenalin to release throughout your body rather than tense up your muscles making you paralytic. But don't get so carried away that you arrive back breathless!

Breath control

You might recall a previous occasion when you had to speak, or were about to when breathing became very difficult, strange and somewhat scary. You can never perform well if that happens, because your breathing controls the oxygen supply to your blood, which feeds your brain, which – I know you appreciate – must be engaged for you to deliver your presentation. Alas, you can't store up oxygen from your morning jog or your brisk walk before you go on. You've got to keep it flowing if you, your body and your brain are going to give a successful performance.

When your nerves get the better of you, your breathing gets shallow, i.e. restricted to the top of your lungs. This kind of breathing is exhausting, forces you to gasp when you speak and causes the pitch of your voice to rise an octave into a shrill, high pitch – something no woman wants. So bear in mind the following tips:

◆ Start by centring your body. If standing, balance yourself evenly on both feet. This aligns your body and allows your vocal cords to work in harmony with your diaphragm and lungs.

◆ Breathe deeply and slowly. Aim to fill the bottom of your lungs first, so your tummy expands. To enable the full use of your powerful and all-important diaphragmatic muscle, don't wear a tight belt or a tight skirt. Let the air rise from the lower to the middle, then upper part of the lungs. You want to feel the air enter your chest almost as if it is blowing up through your throat to your voice.

◆ Take regular, relaxed breaths as you speak. Always breathe in and wait until you are exhaling to begin speaking. Your voice will be deeper and sound more controlled. (Speaking at the beginning of the exhale, or even at the top of the inhale, makes you sound desperate and causes you to gasp. This technique is particularly important when you are being questioned: waiting for the exhale means there will be a natural pauses, for a fleeting few seconds. But the sound that comes out is well worth waiting for, more confident and assured.

Lubricate your vocal cords

♦ Beforehand avoid hot stimulants like tea or coffee especially with milk. Other drinks that don't help are fizzy or very cold ones. It's best to lubricate your voice with warm water containing a slice of lemon or just plain still water (room temperature).

♦ If your voice dries up while you are speaking and no water is available, take a pause and pick up a visual aid or your notes, whatever, seizing the opportunities to chew on your tongue for a few seconds. This will get the saliva going and help to lubricate your throat. But this is a measure to resort to in desperation. You are in charge of the success of your presentation, so should never go on without water readily to hand.

CONSULT THE EXPERTS

If after assiduously practising as recommended earlier, and making your first speeches, you still feel that your voice is hurting your image, consult a good speech therapist. A trained voice coach, speech pathologist or drama coach can assess your problems and recommend specific remedies to help you. Remember that your voice is worth almost 40 per cent of the impact you make, so don't allow yours to let you down unnecessarily.

CHAPTER 11

Your Image across the Table

Meetings are a regular opportunity to present yourself, show what you are worth to superiors and peers in business. Although probably half of them are a complete waste of everyone's time, meetings are how most business gets conducted. Whether you are a participant or the chairperson, how you perform is critical to your career advancement.

In meetings you reveal a lot about yourself and your potential. You show if you have leadership skills, interpersonal skills, communication skills, presentation skills, are on top of your job, can be trusted and relied upon.

Reflect on the regular meetings you attend. Who amongst your colleagues is always very effective? Do they approach every meeting in the same way? If so, what can you learn from them?

GROUP MEETINGS

These can take many forms from regular weekly meetings with subordinates to high-powered, demanding Board meetings – where you may be taking the chair or making your mark as an up and coming new participant. Let's take a look at what you can expect, and need to be prepared for, if you are to be seen at your best.

AS A PARTICIPANT

When you are invited to attend a meeting, make sure you find out the objectives of the chairperson, to help you prepare. Remember, whenever a group is called to discuss one or several issues that means that one individual doesn't have the responsibility to sort things out. Hence, your responsibility in a meeting is shared. You are all individuals contributing different expertise, but in the end must agree on collective solutions. If you play to win or score on points only important to yourself you will become resented and might eventually be excluded from meetings, and once you are no longer at the centre of policy and decision-making, your position will become vulnerable.

Never expect to succeed in a meeting 'on a wing and a prayer'. Preparation is essential. Even if you won't necessarily be called upon to present, swot up on as many issues as possible so that you can contribute. Whenever possible, and without overdoing it, always try to state your views, or ask an intelligent question. Sometimes the chair is very rigid and controls participation, but for normal staff meetings, brainstorming sessions, etc. which make up most of your meetings, try to be actively involved.

WITH SUBORDINATES

Be supportive and encouraging. Supply everyone with an agenda in advance or, if you call the meeting at short notice, let them know its purpose so that they can organise their thoughts and papers ahead of time.

Resist the temptation to finish their sentences or criticise anyone on a personal level, however great the temptation. If you shoot down one the rest will clam-up and you'll get no positive response.

Have someone take minutes or at least note decisions taken and the action points requiring follow-up. Send the minutes out within 24 hours of the meeting, noting exactly who is responsible for following up what.

If the purpose of the meeting is to move a project forward or to get things done, establish a timetable or a date for the next meeting so everyone knows what will be expected of them.

WITH PEERS

Your aim should be seen as collegial but also to earn authority as a leader among equals. For example, the boss will eventually need to find out what the group is thinking, so offer to write up the minutes and submit them to him on behalf of the group.

If an issue on the agenda is yours and central to your interests, don't leave it until the meeting takes place to win agreement. Lobby key people ahead of time; be seen as open to discuss the potential weakness of your proposal, answering as objectively as possible. Even if you are feeling emotional about an objection, never show it. Your detractors will leap on you like a wounded rabbit if they sense a weakness. Instead, keep summarising the benefits of your views and why your proposal meets the objectives set.

WITH SUPERVISORS

Your aim is to be resourceful, and to be seen as collaborating on the objectives.

In these meetings with more senior executives you have an opportunity to shine as well as to be supportive. However, remember that while the **yes person** makes life easy for the chair she wins no reputation as a woman to be given more responsibility. On the other hand, a **prophet of doom** who never makes a good or constructive contribution is also tiresome. If you have reservations or disagree say so, but avoid getting a reputation as someone who always shoots down ideas. Leaders are positive not negative people.

Beware, too, of putting yourself in the role of evaluator on every issue; you may well lend a significant contribution, weighing pros and cons, but should avoid always filling this role; at least occasionally have a decisive view.

Two roles you should never adopt are those of the disrupter or the non-entity:

The **Disrupter** always arrives late or is constantly dashing in and out for messages. This person is just saying that she finds herself superior to the group and that it doesn't merit her attention.

The **Non-Entity** remains part of the furniture; her days are numbered. If you don't/can't participate you are taking up valuable space and will lose your chance to become more involved. More involvement brings more responsibility. More responsibility means more visibility, which means advancement.

AS THE CHAIR

To chair a well run meeting takes preparation plus communication and management skills.

In preparation, always develop an agenda that is as focused as possible. Limit it to one page, preferably no more than a dozen lines in length. Assign presentations ahead of time, getting your key people to lead discussions. Your role is to get the facts out, generate discussion that leads to proposed solutions, evaluate the pros and cons of the solutions and gain agreement on the best one.

Only involve people who are essential and can make a contribution. If the issues require deliberation from a greater number of people, have your managers first go through the same exercise with their teams and then present the concerns and recommendations of their staff in a meeting with you.

Let the participants know what will be expected of them. If you want their input, backup, or research on anything, give them ample notice. Otherwise, a meeting can degenerate into an unwieldy session of off-the-cuff opinions.

Meet in the morning whenever possible, when people are most alert. If the agenda will take all day, better to start very early and allow for a generous lunch break, say one and a half hours, so people have ample time in which to refresh themselves. Encourage a few 10 minute recesses, too, and suggest that people take a walk outside if weather permits.

Choose a meeting room that will be conducive to discussion. One that is too small quickly becomes very claustrophobic; one that is too large and cavernous inhibits discussion.

HOW TO DRESS

Even the most informal brainstorming meeting is a battle ground for status and recognition. To maintain yours or win attention, dress as formally as your normal work environment allows.

If giving a report or presenting, wear an elegant, neutral ensemble (suit or dress with jacket), with just a dash of colour to hold the audience's attention. Very bold colours, like red or yellow, can be overwhelming in a small group if worn overall but can be effective, say, as a blouse to complement a more neutral jacket. Black and navy can be a bit heavy and too sombre on women. Instead, opt for pewter, taupe, olive, purple or camel, to ensure that you will stand out among your dark-suited male colleagues.

WHERE TO SIT

When you arrive at a meeting without assigned seating, it can be a problem figuring out where to sit to achieve your objectives. In some meetings you know you are in for a confrontation with an adversary; in others you need to present and be seen by the greatest number. Then in some meetings you simply want to disappear.

Here are some general guidelines on how to seat yourself strategically:

◆ If you want recognition always sit within good eye contact of the decision-makers (who may not always include the chair).

- If presenting, arrive early and select your best vantage point. At a long table you are best in the middle of one side; at an oval table at one of the narrow curved 'ends'.

- To mitigate a confrontation, sit next to the challenger. It is far more difficult to attack from the side. Avoid sitting directly opposite the person.

- To avoid attention, sit in a 'blind spot' for the chair, your supervisor or the key participant; that is, where it is physically difficult to see you. And wear your most neutral outfit, with no 'special' accessories.

- If you are a junior or new participant, wait to be told where to sit.

POSITIVE BODY LANGUAGE

The BBC once asked me to analyse the dynamics of a corporate staff meeting by watching a video of the proceedings with the volume turned off. It was quite obvious who respected whom, who everyone had no time for, and who was antagonistic towards whom. Do you realise how much *you* expose of your true feelings for colleagues through your behaviour at meetings?

You may be able to control your behaviour in short meetings but longer ones test everyone's patience and inevitably, through fatigue, we begin to send messages loud and clear without even opening our mouths.

You can use your behaviour to impress others or to undermine yourself during meetings. Here's how.

Impressive signals	Undermining signals
Sit upright and alert. Sit forward to convey real interest.	Slouch in your chair.
Keep your eyes on the speaker.	Look down at notes, out of the window, at the ceiling.
Take notes, not constantly, but key points.	Doodle.
Turn your body to the speaker/chair.	Physically turn away.

When listening keep your body 'open': arms leaning forward on the table, relaxed to the sides of your body, hands gently folded.

Fold your arms tightly across your body (says, 'I'm not listening').

Use open gestures: hands open or up as if serving an idea to your colleagues.

Use closed, threatening gestures: like the preaching forefinger to make your points.

Smile and use humour to alleviate tension whenever appropriate.

Deadpan, growling, or cynical expressions.

1

HOW IS YOUR HANDSHAKE?

Your handshake reveals your confidence, professionalism and status. What signals does yours send?
The Patroniser: *(left)* The double-clutch, while often conveying affection or warm feelings, is perceived by many as at best maternal, and at worst patronising
At Arm's Length: *(below left)* A stiff arm fully extended tells others to keep away. You are saying to them that you feel threatened, or that you are aloof and superior to them
Well Met: *(below right)* The correct handshake is direct and friendly. Grip the other person's whole hand with firmness, smile and make direct eye contact

2

3

ONE-TO-ONE : JOB INTERVIEWS

Perhaps the best example of the one-to-one meeting and one most crucial to everyone's career is the job interview. As we are often asked to advise people on what to wear and how to handle themselves in an interview, it merits special discussion here.

The first thing to realise is that the best qualified don't necessarily get the jobs. No, they tend to go to the people most skilled in convincing others that they are right for the job. Even if you don't have all the necessary qualifications and experience, if you want the job and know you can do it, you should be able to sell yourself. You have lots of intangible assets that every employer wants and that can more than compensate for being a bit short on credentials. You may be well-organised, hard-working, able to deal with difficult people. And above all you can exude enthusiasm.

HOW TO DRESS

In the first 3 minutes the interviewer will decide if s/he isn't going to hire you. You should be able to see whether or not the whole exercise is perfunctory after 3 minutes, simply by their behaviour. If you pass the 3 minute hurdle and still note interest, they haven't necessarily decided to hire you, but you do have a chance. That is why your appearance is vital to jumping over that initial hurdle with confidence. Here are some tips:

◆ Make sure you go to bed early the night before, so you are properly rested, and at your best.

◆ Wear the best suit you can afford or borrow and make sure it is pressed. Check that you can sit down in it comfortably without the skirt riding up. If you know you look good, you will have more self-confidence.

◆ Choose neutral rather than loud colours but show more flair if applying to a creative industry.

◆ Look current but never trendy (unless in the fashion business). If you are aiming to return to work after starting a family, don't wear anything 'mumsie'.

◆ Avoid flashy scarves or accessories.

◆ Don't wear perfume.

◆ Aim for understated elegance.

◆ Shoes must match your suit in quality, and be well-polished. Court shoes are the safest style; don't wear stillettos, flats or boots.

- Sport an elegant attaché or leather file; if you have neither, see if you can borrow one.

- If it is a rainy day and you're carrying an umbrella, make sure it tones with your outfit and is not overly large.

- Use a neat, small note pad and a good quality fountain pen to take notes.

- Always wear make-up, naturally in soft colours.

- Cover any spots with concealer.

- Have clean hair. Avoid greasy gels, the wet-look or outlandish styles. Tie-back or put up long hair. Don't use childish ribbons or tie-backs. Aim for a classic simplicity.

- Have clean, manicured nails which will be on view as you take notes. Do not wear brightly coloured nail-varnish. Use a natural varnish or simply buff your nails to achieve a healthy sheen.

- Keep jewellery to a minimum but wear significant earrings.

- Leave your coat in reception.

HOW TO BEHAVE

What you say in an interview is important, but how you speak and your general behaviour are also under scrutiny. In addition to finding out if you can actually do the job, the interviewer is probing to see how you will fit into the corporate culture.

- Be enthusiastic without going overboard.

- Shake hands upon meeting the interviewer and look him/her straight in the eye, with a smile. Shake hands again on leaving.

- Sit relaxed in the chair but don't slump. Don't sit too far forward unless in a very soft chair/sofa. (See also hints on body language given in Chapter 11.)

- Don't become too relaxed, even if you think things are going well. Think 'professional'. Never, for instance, smoke – don't even consider asking if you can!

- Don't joke around aside from pleasantries or the odd witticism. No one wants a clown, unless that's the job you are applying for.

- Take a pen and note pad out at the beginning of the interview and jot down a few notes throughout. This shows interest and also attention to details but don't make them so copious that you can't give the interviewer due attention.

◆ If the interviewer takes a phone call that is running on, after a few minutes take out an article from your attaché or brief-case and begin reading it. You will avoid looking like an unwilling eavesdropper, and reading a business article will help you to look intelligent and show that you don't waste time.

The job interview is like a sales call, except that you are the only product you've got. Don't expect one act to go down the same with all interviewers. They are all different. You need to have sharp, honest, positive replies to all the standard questions like:

◆ 'Why are you interested in this job?'

◆ 'Why are you leaving your present job?'

◆ 'Why were you made redundant?'

◆ 'What experience are you most proud of in your career thus far?'

◆ 'What are your strengths? Weaknesses?'

◆ 'You have different (or no) experience. How can you do this job?'

◆ 'Why should we hire you?'

◆ 'What are your outside interests?'

Answers to these and similar questions you need to have prepared. But never jump to answer the questions. Take your time. Answer only as you are exhaling.

Size up the interviewer. What response did s/he like best and why? Some people like examples of your experiences explained; others want to see examples of what you did. Some want you to be brief, others like you to elaborate. *Listen to* and *observe* the interviewer and give her/him what s/he likes, how s/he likes it.

If you don't prove to be the lucky candidate in your earliest interviews, at least you'll learn through practice and discover how to project yourself in your best light. Remember, those who seem most polished at interviewing are only former students of the art who have studied and practised. You can succeed, too, if you make the effort.

CHAPTER 12

In the Public Eye

If you are particularly resourceful and successful in your career, sooner or later you might be asked to speak on behalf or your organisation, perhaps even to represent it under the scrutiny of the media. The first opportunity to stand in the limelight often produces a 'fight or flight' response, particularly in the untrained. Nervous about being interviewed, you argue your position defensively, unaware of how belligerent and underconfident you appear. Or you are so desperate to get the interview over that you race through your replies, giving inadequate attention to the questions and insufficient thought to what you are saying.

Even the most capable, articulate manager can appear incompetent if unprepared for an encounter with an inquisitive journalist. Hence, it is wise to think through how you can handle being in the Public Eye, especially if you ever consider choosing a public life.

TELEVISION

Handling the media, particularly television, takes a different set of skills that most of us have to learn. Few can 'wing' an interview with no training or preparation and come off well. We have all witnessed punters make fools of themselves on television. You know, the news report where the unsuspecting company spokes-person was sent into the studio ill-prepared and poorly-groomed for a tough interview. It is embarrassing to watch when a no doubt normally articulate and nice person comes off either as a crook or an idiot.

TV is an art-form, and you need to learn the rules of the game in order to present yourself and your case with success. Your company will blame you for foolhardiness, rather than praise you for your brave effort, if you put up a woeful performance… and you almost certainly won't ever get another opportunity. So be prepared.

PREPARING FOR A TV INTERVIEW

As when preparing for a successful large audience presentation, you have to do your homework before any TV interview. Just knowing you will be discussing a particular issue isn't enough.

Research the following:

◆ What kind of programme will you be on? There's a world of difference between hard news and a chat show. Sometimes they will discuss the same issue but the treatment is light years apart.

◆ How much time do you have for your interview? The researcher should tell you this quite precisely. For example, you might be part of a 5 minute piece but only be likely to be asked one or two questions, and get only a minute of air time.

◆ Who else will be appearing with you? Expect the format to include a protagonist (possibly yourself) and an antagonist (possibly a competitor, disgruntled employee, irate customer, union official, consumer activist, politician, etc.). If no one else is part of the interview, expect your interviewer to be the 'devil's advocate'.

◆ Who is the interviewer? You might be familiar with the programme but interviewers are usually working on a rota basis; so check who will be on duty. Once known, watch him/her beforehand or ask the researcher for tapes of a couple of their previous interviews, to get a sense of their style and interview technique.

◆ Where will the interview be held? An in-studio appearance requires different preparation from one on location, say, at your office. If the latter, never agree to begin filming until you have checked exactly how you will be positioned. Ask to see the monitor before you begin and eliminate anything distracting or likely to be misinterpreted.

HANDLING THE INTERVIEW

If asked to be interviewed on television, make sure you have your own objectives very clear. You will be hit with all sorts of questions, some irrelevant to the central message you need and want to convey. Your main worry should never be the interviewer but the clock. Time is always of the essence. So your message must be concise, effective and premeditated.

Your message

Focus your message to a few key points, kept simple but reinforced by everything you say.

If you are brought in to defend a charge, whether or not fairly levied, decide ahead of time how you will respond. Write out the reply and practise it on others before the interview. Be positive, own-up if needed (having first established with your company executives that this *is* a possibility and your reaction must be prepared), present remedies and, above all, be pleasant. Even if you have been boxed into a tight corner and you are on the defensive, try not to look or sound it; *never* lose your temper.

In some situations, an interview can be vital to business, if not a turning point one way or another in your career. If in doubt at all about your ability to tackle tough questions and defend your position, have colleagues rehearse likely questions ahead of time so you get your message flowing smoothly. After all, you are representing them, and you have every right to expect their support.

The interviewer

Believe it or not, s/he is human, too. Many first-time interviewees are terrified by their potential interviewer. They have the edge over you in being familiar with the technology, the set and the main questions they will put to you. But you have the edge with your expertise which they need, and they cannot always anticipate your responses so they, too, have to think on their feet.

Never project signals that convey you feel inferior to the interviewer. S/he is no doubt highly intelligent and well-briefed, but s/he isn't the specialist that you are in your field. Treat the interviewer neither as a superior nor an inferior, but as your professional equal.

However much you may be provoked, keep your composure and never attack back. The interviewer is familiar to the audience. You are the outsider who can become the *antagonist* if you show any hostility. Keep your answer brief and to the point. If you have to dig, do so with a genial smile on your face to take the sting out of a tough reply. Your goal is to appear open, competent and trustworthy.

YOUR TV IMAGE

If you expect an increasing role in television, it is wise to get some professional coaching ahead of time. It is essential for you to see for yourself how you come across under questioning, as well as to see how you look. Mock TV interviews on video are illuminating, not soul destroying. They give most people greater confidence in handling the real thing, especially if talked through an analysis of their strong and weak points by a professional.

Short of being able to receive such coaching before an important interview, here are some general guidelines to help you handle your first television appearance with success.

EFFECTIVE COLOURS

Time now to learn what sort of clothing is most effective on camera. We've all watched the pretty presenter in fuchsia pink with matching lipstick and been struck by how we couldn't listen to a word she was saying have been mesmerised by her fuchsia lips!

Certain colours are enhancing on camera and others are not:

◆ Avoid extremes like very light or dark colours. Black is overwhelming on camera while white bleaches out and has a blinding effect.

◆ Strong pinks, such as magenta through to red, defy focusing in most studios and have an effect known as 'bleeding', that is, the outlines get fuzzy and seem to run, like a dye.

◆ The more sophisticated the set the better able it is to handle strong colours. Assume that your local news station or the satellite studio is ill-equipped and avoid problem colours.

◆ The easiest colours on camera are those in the middle of the colour spectrum: blues, greens and purples. These are focused easily and come up the truest on camera. The blue-greens and turquoise shades are especially attractive.

◆ For blues try: medium blue, royal, french or grey-blue, periwinkle (violet/blue), light navy or teal blue.

◆ The greens that look wonderful range from moss and olive to emerald. (Deep greens like forest look black while bright greens can be blinding.)

◆ Purples look elegant on camera, ranging from medium lilac, violet, soft plum to purple. (Again, beware of very deep purple which turns muddy or black on television.

Consider the set when selecting what to wear. Many today are very colourful and require specific colours (out of the ones recommended above) simply for contrast. The more neutral the set the more colourful you can be. If the programme on which you are to appear does not have a regular set, ring the studio and ask for details. At the same time, ask for specific advice on the most appropriate colours. It is in their interests, too, to tell you.

EFFECTIVE STYLES

Plain styles are best to wear on television. A well-cut jacket with a clean neckline is far more effective than a patterned ensemble which might start strobing on camera. Watch the female presenters on news programmes and compare their styles to those on 'light entertainment' or magazine shows. The news presenters generally wear more simple, 'forgettable' clothes while those of women presenting more fun programmes are generally unforgettable! You have a message to project, so be sure your clothes are simple, attractive and don't distract from what you are saying.

The neckline is critical. If your neck is short, don't clutter it with a high fussy collar or chunky necklace. Keep the neckline open and simple, either a jewel or V-neck. Shorter hairstyles will be more flattering on camera for you.

If you have a long neck, you can appear severe and gawky if you leave it completely exposed on camera. Soften the effect by tucking into the jacket collar a scarf (solid colour, no patterns). In lieu of a scarf, fill the neckline with a choker or necklace. A turned-up collar is another good effect. Wear your hair longer, to soften the neck area; shoulder length works well.

BBC's Moira Stuart looks both elegant and professional in a plain jacket with a simple, clean neckline. All the focus is on her news report. For 'lighter' programmes you can wear more colour and add a few accessories. But remember that less is always best

If you feel a plain jacket is too boring, that is, in a neutral colour and without any special features, add a necklace or brooch in matt gold, silver or pearls for interest. Avoid diamanté or coloured stones. Earrings should never be 'drop' style (another great distraction). And if your trademark is an armful of bangle bracelets, remove them before going on camera or the soundmen will murder you.

MAKE-UP FOR TELEVISION

No one – male or female – appears on television without make-up. You need it just to look polished, healthy and *human* under the harsh set lights. Don't leave your arrival at the studios so late that you don't have time to visit the make-up artist. And never agree to go on camera without being made up by an expert, unless you know from long experience how to prepare yourself.

People believe that you need to wear a lot of heavy make-up to look good on TV. The opposite is true. Though you do need foundation, concealer, powder, blusher, mascara and lipstick, all the colours must be matt, subtle and natural – never pearlised, bright or too dark.

American TV presenters distinguish themselves around the world by wearing lip gloss over their lipstick. To Europeans, this looks very garish and concentrates viewers attention on the lips, when you want it on your eyes. So don't adopt this habit.

My advice for looking wonderful on camera is:

Foundation
If your skin is uneven in colour and patchy in texture, you'll need a slightly heavier base than usual. A water-based foundation might not be enough. Try a cream base for better coverage.

Choose a colour one shade darker than your natural skintone. Normally, you match your skintone (i.e. for everyday make-up). But you can look very pale and drawn under strong studio lights if you don't enhance your skintone modestly.

Concealer
It's essential to lighten up under the eyes, even if your dark circles 'aren't too bad'. Overhead studio lights can often make these dark areas very dark so always lighten up your eye area with concealer.

Translucent powder
A light dusting with a big brush isn't enough. Press the powder in gently with a powder puff. You might look a bit 'floury' immediately afterwards

but your skin will soon absorb it and within minutes you'll look fine.

Eye-shadows

No 'colour-colours' like blues or greens. Soft browns teamed with a natural highlighter such as soft pink or apricot are best. Greys make you look as if you got punched the night before, so stick to the soft browns ranging from cocoa and pewter to honey and neutral brown.

Eye pencil and mascara

Define your eyes gently on the outer third of the upper and lower lids with a soft kohl pencil, but never use black. Try a neutral brown, spruce green, navy or plum, whichever best complements your eyes.

Use mascara on the top lashes only, and liberally but not thickly. Apply a thin layer (black or brown only). Let this dry and comb through. Apply a second layer if you want to enhance their thickness or lengthen them.

Eyebrows

Fill out the overall shape with a soft brown eye-shadow, applied with gentle dabs of a short-haired brush. This looks more natural than pencil lines. Finish by brushing up with a comb coated with hair gel.

Blusher

Be very easy-handed here. Use only a natural tone that compliments your colouring type. Salmon, terracotta, and a dusty rose are best. Blend really well so that it looks as natural as possible.

Lipstick

As you won't be wearing red or strong pinks on camera, go for a soft, non-pearlised, neutral shade. A well-known make-up artist at CBS TV in America recommends using a colour that matches the inside of your lip. I think you are safe to be a bit more colourful than that.

First powder your lips lightly, to help the lipstick take more effectively. Try a natural base of soft mauve, mahogany, tan pink or wine and then add a dash of a brighter salmon or cool pink to the centre of the top and lower lips and blend well.

Be sure to retouch your powder (see opposite) and lipstick if you are left a long time between having your make-up done and going on camera. A good trick for drinking coffee or water without messing your lipstick is to lick the cup at the spot where you intend to drink, before taking a sip. The wet surface prevents your lipstick from sticking to the cup.

HAIR FOR TELEVISION

An attractive hairstyle is vital to a good TV image. Your hair frames your face, so assess very carefully how well the shape, colour and texture of your own hair works for you, particularly on camera. Hairstyles that seem perfectly OK in everyday life, can be disastrous on television.

Ask yourself right now: if you had to appear on TV tonight, how do you think your hair would look? Professional women need to settle on a style that they can easily maintain themselves between four to six weekly visits to a good hairdresser. If you are blessed with beautifully thick and long hair, are you skilled in pulling it up or back? If not, a smart shoulder-length style that can be controlled with hair gel or spray is recommended.

For TV, your hair should frame, not overwhelm, your face. Depending on the programme, you should adapt your hairstyle, and whole appearance, to look appropriate to your audience. If you are on a news programme, the style shouldn't be excessively contrived or fussy. For a magazine format or chat show, a severe, simple style isn't glamorous enough.

Colour is very important to the success of a woman's hairstyle. Often, natural, uncoloured hair can look dead and mousey on camera, even if it looks lovely in real life. If you don't wish to colour your hair, you might try a semi-permanent rinse close to your own natural colouring, simply to give it some vibrancy prior to a TV appearance.

If you already colour your hair, be scrupulous about the state of your roots. Bleached blondes especially beware. If you don't pay care to touching up your roots you will look as if your hair is dirty – even though it may be squeaky clean. So book an appointment with your colourist before you appear on TV, if you have time.

If you have grey hair don't consider colouring it just for TV. Soft grey tones, and even vibrant salt and pepper hair, are lovely on television.

It's the very artificial dyed tones of blonde, red and orange that can look horribly artificial on TV. The softer ash highlights for blondes and chestnut tones for brunettes are more flattering. A redhead, who is so naturally, always looks wonderful on TV.

GLASSES

All too often, amateurs appear on TV in ill-fitted, unstylish frames and without a protective coating on the lenses to deflect the glare of studio lights. Such spectacles would hurt anyone's chances of communicating effectively.

But many people are simply uncomfortable without their eyeglasses. Despite how much younger and better looking Prime Minister John

Major is without his they are his security blanket. And many people, male and female, feel this way. Some, indeed, are enhanced by well-chosen frames; others, who do not need glasses, wear frames containing clear glass simply because they feel that the glasses give them a more mature, authoritative look. And there are many spectacle wearers who would prefer the option of wearing contact lenses, but for various reasons cannot.

If you must wear eyeglasses on TV, choose a pair that are flattering. On television your spectacles should not be so fashionable or fussy that they actually wear you rather than the reverse. So keep the colour of the frames neutral, with a clear bridge and your eyes at the centre of the lens.

CONTACT LENSES

Many professionals have opted for contact lenses to make them look more natural or younger. If you are hard on your glasses and generally treat them badly so that they get scratched and bent easily, or lose them often enough to have expensive replacement bills, then maybe contact lenses are a better option than glasses.

Your optometrist will advise whether or not your individual sight impairment will be conducive to lenses. Then you have the choice of clear or coloured versions. There are literally hundreds of shades to consider even to turn brown eyes blue. Obviously, lenses that are painted are opaque and achieve the most dramatic coverage. But the effect of opaque-coloured lenses can freak some people as the effect is so unnatural that your eyes take over your image and inhibit communication. So, if you are interested in changing or enhancing the natural colour of your eyes, opt for translucent ones that will have everyone guessing.

Remember, if you have lenses in different colours it will cause havoc with your wardrobe and make-up. The colour of your eyes is key to what colours in clothes, hair colour and make-up will be most flattering. Ivana Trump sports about a half dozen different coloured contact lenses, but she, perhaps unlike you, has the budget to maintain that many separate wardrobes! So if considering a major change of eye colour don't under-estimate the other major investments required subsequently to go with your new image.

BODY LANGUAGE

In addition to all the essential grooming already detailed, there are a few other considerations before you are truly ready for the interview, to ensure you are seen and heard to your best advantage.

Posture

Many TV sets are furnished with low, comfortably cushioned sofas or chairs. These are a disaster for most TV novices, who automatically sit upon them as they would at home, well back and sunken. You lose all your energy and credibility when you sit naturally in a chair or sofa on TV. The whole experience is unnatural; so, too, must be your posture.

Sit at the edge of your chair, leaning very slightly forward, with your back as straight as possible. If you are small and find the seat you are offered makes you lower than the presenter, request a higher chair with a firm seat. If this is not easily accepted as a very reasonable request, insist. Yes, insist! You are the guest and you are there at their request. They should have the courtesy to treat you as a guest. And it is in the interests of the programme that you are clearly visible! So make sure the conditions are as favourable as possible in order for you to put in a good appearance and come off well.

Facial expressions and gestures

The atmosphere of a TV studio is daunting and not user-friendly. All sorts of equipment is jutting in from above and below, and a busy cast of assistants are around to prod you with microphones, move you about and direct you. It is only natural to freeze up amid all the activity and to look like a deer caught in a car's headlights as soon as you appear on camera.

Take a few good deep breaths before sitting down (slightly forward and back straight) and smile at the presenter. Don't be distracted by the cameras or attempt to talk directly to any one of them. You are speaking with an interviewer and, possibly, other guests; try to imagine yourself having this conversation in your home or at your office. Even so, don't allow yourself to relax: remember, you must keep to your message and try to come off as positively as possible.

If the subject is a serious one, you'll look simple-minded if you smile throughout the interview. Your aim is to look serious and credible but not severe. However, do flash an occasional smile if an appropriate opportunity arises, so that the viewers warm to you.

Light-hearted interviews require almost a constant smile, even if this doesn't come naturally to you. My mouth, like many, turns down at the corners. So when I'm expressionless, I can actually look annoyed. For me it's agony, but I put on an effective smile for TV interviews and end up looking only pleasant, not the idiot that I feel inside. Most of today's presenters are hired in part for their looks. And a key factor to their looks is their smile. They all have mouths that turn upwards!

In addition to maintaining eye contact with your interviewer, looking pleasant and sitting forward, you also must use gestures which are open. When some guests are nervous they cross their arms to hug themselves, which projects a defensive person. And if seated behind a table or desk don't think that by keeping your hands below the table you are kidding anyone that you're not secretly wringing them together! Keep them visible; you look unnatural without your hands.

It is best to keep your hands folded together to start with if you are nervous but gradually to open them and use them to help you express your points. But don't wave them about wildly – it does happen sometimes on TV when guests get carried away by their own enthusiasm and it can be very irritating for the viewer. Hands can also appear disproportionately large if they are thrust forward towards the camera! Avoid the teacher's preaching forefinger or aggressive mid-air slicing to emphasise points. Keep your palms up or slightly angled to the sides to project that you are visibly offering a position for consideration. And always make sure, before going on the set, that your hands and nails are as well-groomed as the rest of you.

CHAPTER 13

Choosing a Public life

A successful career sometimes brings opportunities to become involved in community affairs, from ad hoc, voluntary roles, such as being a charity worker, or serving on a school board or hospital committee, to holding an elected public office on a part-time or possibly even a full-time basis.

Politicians, in particular, know that they must be as concerned with image as they are with substance if they wish to have a successful, long-term career in public life. Even those who publicly deny that image is important, fearing that people will think that they aren't serious about their jobs, privately focus as much attention on the presentation as on the formulation of public policy. They know that this is the professional approach required in modern politics. The politician is the vehicle for explaining issues and proposing solutions; that vehicle packages the message and becomes the message itself.

Anyone in public life, be they a single-issue activist or elected official, appreciates the all-importance of televised communication. Either they master it or they fade into obscurity. Television is a career-maker and a career-breaker. Parties and leaders that use it effectively win, those who don't lose.

In America, television was first used in the public arena to cover a Congressional investigation into organised crime in the 1950s. It turned the chairman of the proceedings, a self-deprecating, southern Senator Estes Kefauver into a cult figure. Later, during the 1960 Presidential election between John F. Kennedy and the then Vice President, Richard Nixon, the first such 'candidates' debates' on TV proved defeating for the arguably more experienced and better briefed Vice President. Preferring to rely on such political advantages, Nixon failed to groom himself for television, wearing the wrong colours and refusing outright any make-up – and he lost to the young up-start Kennedy because the latter looked more convincing to the American public on television. Kennedy had not only been dressed appropriately and had asked to be made-up, prior to appearing on TV, but also was coached in handling his body language and gestures to look more capable, to look like a winner.

All leading figures in modern politics have had their image advisors; not simply to write their memorable speeches but to teach them acting skills to enhance their delivery, and guidance in 'power dressing'. Harold MacMillan underwent a total overhaul as Prime Minister, with the advent of television into British politics. US President Lyndon Johnson, not remembered for his good looks, had extra inches added to his shirt collars to hide his distracting Adam's apple. President Jimmy Carter donned woolly cardigans for his fireside chats to Americans during the energy crisis in the late 1970s, to urge people to turn their thermostats down and to bundle up inside – just as he and his family did at the White House.

Everyone worldwide watched with fascination the gradual but profound transformation of Britain's first woman Prime Minister. Everything from how Mrs. Thatcher spoke – she was coached to lower her voice and to speak more deliberately – to the colour and styling of her hair, make-up and clothes was fine-tuned before our eyes.

Even Thatcher's successor, Britain's self-confessed 'plug-ugly' John Major, has taken advice. It is hard to believe, but his charmingly non-descript image has been discreetly revamped. The sombre grey suits have been replaced by quality Chester Barries, the ties are a little less conservative, his blue shirts which emphasised his beard line are now pink or soft white, and a non-reflective coating has been added to the lenses of his glasses. The impact of these changes has been modest but it's as far as Mr. Major is willing to go – for the moment.

POLITICIANS' PARTNERS

Political spouses, generally wives, are increasingly subjected to comment about their images and how they help or detract from the nation's image abroad. The wives even get photographed together and scored according to their standing in the style stakes.

First Lady Hillary Clinton had to undergo a substantial make-over during the 1992 Presidential campaign because her severe 'career woman' image was costing her husband votes. Functional glasses were replaced with contact lenses, her naturally mousey hair was highlighted golden

Hillary Clinton before her substantial make-over (left) and after (right)

blonde and her rather shapeless suits replaced by more figure-hugging knits. She even submitted her recipe for brownies against that of incumbent Barbara Bush and, surprisingly, won.

DEVELOPING A PUBLIC IMAGE

If you are interested in preparing yourself for any role in public life it is wise to consider what you need to change before you are in the limelight. The last thing you want is for your image to become an issue – for it to appear that you need a 'going-over' in order to be more appealing to your public. A good public image may not be the main reason why you get the job, but it will help you be listened to and possibly believed in. A good image bridges gaps with people of different backgrounds, of different ages, and that is crucial whether you are a politician, a sales representative or, say, a charity worker.

The first challenge in developing an image that will work for, not against you in public life is to remove or resolve any distractions. These might include a too distinctive hair-style, a gap in your teeth, looking unfit, or using irritating, habitual gestures. A poor quality voice is another great disadvantage that needs to be improved.

IMAGE ADVICE

Audit your physical appearance

If you can't be objective about your appearance get others to tell you what two or three things need dealing with to help improve your image.

Pay attention to your face, in particular, as this will be the focus of your television interviews. Is your grooming first-rate? Is your skin in good condition or would it benefit from occasional facials?

Visit the dental hygienist three times a year, to keep your teeth as white as possible. Consider having bad teeth improved by cosmetic dentistry, such as capping.

The eyes have it

Your eyes are vital to your effectiveness as a communicator. Are yours shown in the best possible light? Always define them with kohl pencil and soft eye-shadow, and accentuate your eyebrows. Always wear mascara. Tweeze or wax away unsightly hairs between your brows to look more groomed. Be sure your glasses are tinted with a non-reflective coating but not colour tinted, as this would hide your eyes.

Not a hair out of place

If your hair is unruly and difficult to control, see a good stylist to advise you on a better cut, and possibly a soft perm or any other necessary treatment to make it more manageable. If you are going grey, and it isn't flattering, consider a rinse closer to your natural colour. Use hairspray every day, if your hair is fine, to keep it in place. If you have a good head of hair worn in a short style, use a little gel, rubbed between your two hands then lightly 'brushed' through your hair to keep it in place but still allow movement.

Get fit!

A lumpy, lethargic person can't fake fitness by simply picking up their pace when in the public eye. You need to be trim (*not* necessarily slim!) for your size, and show a vigour that only comes from eating well and getting enough rest and exercise. Far too many public figures allow their schedules to be punishing. Such self-abuse eventually makes itself evident, so be in control of your life. Build both exercise and rest into your daily diary.

If you do become run down, try to get away to a health farm for at least a weekend and allow yourself to unwind and be pampered. Or, at least, resolve to leave your work problems behind for the weekend and treat yourself to a couple of days of total relaxation. And do just that.

Show some personality

Whenever you're making a public appearance, avoid looking like a clone of anyone else. Always wear a dash of colour unless the occasion is very serious.

Look approachable

If you represent a public group or company of any kind, look as if people could actually come up to you and ask a question or have a conversation. Don't look so serious, or take yourself so seriously that you put off the very people you wish to attract.

Always be aware of how you sit, your gestures and your facial expressions. Don't sit ramrod straight; move forward, shift slightly, tilt your head when you are supposed to be listening and smile whenever you have the opportunity, when it is appropriate to do so. Touch people when you meet them – not allowing excessive bear-hugs or kisses – but offering a forthright handshake, a touch on the upper arm, softly squeezing a hand to show that you really reach out to people. A simple touch conveys that individual people matter to you and they will respond accordingly.

If you are asked to appear on weekend TV for an interview, don't appear in a business suit. Real people at home watching you are probably in casual wear. You can't appear in a tracksuit, unless participating in some sporting event, but you can and should 'dress down'. Try a casual skirt and pretty blouse, or, if trousers suit you and are more your style, try an elegant pair with a colourful knit top. Your make-up and grooming must still be first-rate.

CONCLUSION

'To Thine Own Self be True'

There you have it. All our up-to-date advice on how to present the best of yourself in your career. I hope that you will try out at least some of the many suggestions contained in this book. For unless you evaluate honestly who you are today and how you come across to others, defining the areas in which you need to improve your image, how are you to grow? You can't expect others to appreciate your abilities, if you deny them yourself by projecting an image that suggests only negative things about you.

I hope that you will now have a sense of direction and a list of priority steps to take. Maybe you will sign-up for a Presentation Skills course to confront your fear of public speaking, having learned how vital it is further in your career. Perhaps you will have the inspiration to smarten up an indifferent wardrobe, realising that your clothes simply aren't doing you justice. With the guidelines you now have on selecting colours and styles, and building a co-ordinating wardrobe you can easily recreate your image within your own budget. It needn't cost a fortune, if you follow my advice.

I trust you accept that even though your image may have worked fairly well for you thus far, it might not be what's needed to help you in the future. Fine-tuning is needed throughout your career. So don't ever rest on your laurels. Do something about those weaknesses in your own image, those roadblocks to further success.

Above all, remember that the packaging and the art of presenting yourself must be true to the real you inside. A new image won't turn you into someone else; it *will* make more of you, *who you are*. An improved image will give you a tremendous boost in confidence. But it is up to you to see the job through.

If my advice helps to get you through doors previously closed to you, over hurdles you would never have contemplated jumping and, most importantly, feeling better about yourself, then I will consider my efforts to have been worthwhile. I wish you well.

Bibliography

PRESENTATION SKILLS

Janner's Complete Speechmaker, Greville Janner, QC, MP (Century Business)
How To Talk So People Listen, Sonya Hamlin (Thorsons)
Never Be Nervous Again, Dorothy Sarnoff (Crown Books, NY)
Personal Power, Philippa Davies (Piatkus)
Power Communication Skills, Dr. Susan Baile (Career Track Publications, NY)
Power Presentations, Brody and Kent (Wiley)
Powerspeak, Dorothy Leeds (Piatkus)

HANDLING TV

Communications and the Modern World, Ken Ward (Macmillan)
Understanding Media, Marshall McLuhan (Ark Paperbacks)
You Are The Message, Roger Ailes and John Krausmar (Dow Jones-Irwin)
Your Public Best, Lillian Brown (New Market Press)

CAREER DEVELOPMENT.

A Passion for Excellence, Tom Peters (Warner Books, NY)
A Passion for Leadership, Tom Peters (Warner Books, NY)
Breaking the Glass Ceiling, Ann Morrison, etc., Center for Creative Leadership (Addison-Wesley, USA)
The 7 Habits of Highly Effective People, Stephen R Covey (Simon & Schuster)

CORPORATE IMAGE

Corporate Identity, Wally Olins (Thames & Hudson)
The Business of Image, Nicholas Jenkins (Kogan Page)

WOMEN'S IMAGE

Body Traps, Dr Judith Rodin (William Morrow, NY)
The Color Me Beautiful Make-Up Book, Carol Jackson (Piatkus Books)
The Complete Style Guide, Mary Spillane (Piatkus Books)
Discover Your Colours Video from Color Me Beautiful
   (Chrysalis Home Video)
It's You, Emily Cho (Villard Books)
The Professional Image, Susan Bixler (Putnam)
Wardrobe, Susie Faux (Piatkus Books)

PUBLIC IMAGE

Images of Power, Brendan Bruce (Kogan Page)

CROSS CULTURAL UNDERSTANDING

Eurobarometer: Public Opinion in the European Community
   (published by the EC)
Culturgram for the 90s, Brigham Young University, Center for
   International Studies, Provo, Utah
Going International, Lennie Copeland and Lewis Griggs (Penguin, NY)
Guide des Bonnes Mannières et du Protocole en Europe, Jacques
   Gandouin (Fixot)
Mind Your Manners, John Mole (The Industrial Society, London)
The Art of Japanese Management, Pascale and Athos (Simon and
   Schuster, NY)
*The Travellers Guide to Middle Eastern and North African Customs
   and Manners*, E. Devine and N. Braganti (St. Martin's Press, NY)
The World Class Executive, Neil Chesanow (Rawson Associates, NY)

Picture Credits

page 26: dresses and jacket by Marks & Spencer, earrings, bangles and bracelet by Kenneth Jay Lane, scarf by Color Me Beautiful

page 29: photo courtesy of The Body Shop plc

pages 40, 42, 44, 46, 48, 50: photographs © Rex Features

page 53, *top left:* blouse and blazer by Next, earrings by Kenneth Jay Lane; *top right:* blouse and jacket by Marks & Spencer; *bottom left:* jacket by Nicol Fahri, blouse by Next, necklace and earrings by Kenneth Jay Lane;

bottom right: jacket by Next, scarf by Color Me Beautiful, earrings and brooch by Kenneth Jay Lane;

page 72, left: skirt and jumper by Pallant, jacket by Vertigo, earrings and necklace by Kenneth Jay Lane;

centre: top by Jaeger; right: trousers by Sonia Rykiel, bag by Marks & Spencer, waistcoat by Tom Gilbey

page 75, *left:* dress by Next, shoes by Marks & Spencer, earrings by Kenneth Jay Lane; *right:* skirt, top, shoes and attaché by Marks & Spencer, earrings by Kenneth Jay Lane;

page 77, *left:* shoes by Marks & Spencer; right: shoes by Bally

page 79, left and centre: skirt by Next, top by Marks & Spencer; *right:* jacket by Next, scarf by Color Me Beautiful, earrings by Kenneth Jay Lane

page 81: jackets and trousers by Marks & Spencer

page 82, *top:* waistcoat and trousers by Marks & Spencer; *bottom left:* suit by Fabrice Karel; *bottom right:* cardigan and skirt by Marks & Spencer, earrings and chain by Kenneth Jay Lane

page 86, *left:* dress and jacket by Marks & Spencer; *right:* dress by Marks & Spencer, scarf by Color Me Beautiful, earrings and brooch by Kenneth Jay Lane

page 93: skirt and top by Marks & Spencer

page 95: shoes by Bally

page 99: 1. twinset by Marks & Spencer 2. jacket and blouse by Next, earrings by World Gold Council 3. as 2. above, with scarf by Color Me Beautiful

page 103: photographs courtesy Dentics, cosmetic dental studios and shops, (telephone 071 730 5780)

page 114, *top:* photograph © Telegraph Colour Library; *bottom:* photograph © Tony Stone Photolibrary London

page 118: photograph © Tony Stone Photolibrary London

page 129: he wears suit by Hugo Boss at Austin Reed, she wears jacket and skirt by JH Collectibles at Selfridges, and scarf from Options at Austin Reed

page 137: photograph © BBC News and Current Affairs

page 146: photographs © Rex Features

Index

Page numbers in italic refer to the illustrations.

MORE FROM CMB IMAGE CONSULTANTS

YOUR PERSONAL COLOUR SWATCHES

You can order our handy shopping guide to your best colours by requesting information about our Personal Colour Swatches. You will receive a set of over 30 fabric swatches representing your 'Dominant Colour' type as identified in this book. The colour wallet can help you sort out your existing wardrobe as well as avoid future shopping mistakes.

PERSONAL IMAGE CONSULTATIONS

CMB's top image consultants can offer more advice on your image so you feel confident that you are presenting yourself at your best.

An individual consultation will show you colours and styles for work as well as casual wear and how to combine colours and patterns to achieve a look that works for you.

Our aim is to make selecting clothes easy. You receive your own style guide full of notes as well as a wallet of 60 colour fabric swatches to use when shopping. To put the theory into practice, or for women with time restrictions, CMB can organise individual shopping trips.

CMB PRODUCTS

CMB offers exclusive ranges of cosmetics, skincare products, scarves and fashion accessories. If you are interested, tick the box on the Information Request form for a copy of our catalogue.

CMB SEMINARS ON PROJECTING SUCCESS

For organisations keen to present their best image, CMB conduct corporate training seminars in personal image, etiquette and presentation.

For further details on our services or products, please complete and return the freepost information request form below. Alternatively, ring us directly on 071 627 5211

CMB Image Consultants, 66 Abbey Business Centre, Ingate Place, London SW8 3NS

INFORMATION REQUEST FORM

Please send me information on the following:

(tick the boxes as necessary)   **My Personal Colour Swatches**   ☐

Personal Image Consultation   ☐

CMB's Product Catalogue   ☐

CMB's Corporate Seminars   ☐

NAME:_____ *(please print)*

ADDRESS: _____

_____

DAYTIME TELEPHONE NO: _____